50 YEARS LATER

Midwood's High School Reunion a School from Which I Never Graduated

Ron Salmonson

ISBN: 1523612878
ISBN 13: 9781523612871

ACKNOWLEDGMENTS

This book wouldn't have been given life without the loving support of my wife, Iris, who encouraged me again to put these recollections, confessions, and thoughts on paper. Iris spent hours assisting the editing by reading and rereading the drafts that preceded this final version. In addition, her computer skills more than facilitated its publication.

I also would like to thank the weekly writing club at Valencia Falls in Delray Beach, Florida, where we winter, for making my ideas less weak. I appreciate each member of the group but especially recognize Howard Gleichenhaus, Joyce Saltman, Jeanne Freedman, and Stan Bogaty.

I am also indebted to the many friends and patients, too numerous to mention, who've read some of these excerpts and encouraged me to publish these passages so that others may read.

Thanks goes out to my lifelong friends, Gary Harrison, from kindergarten, and Michael Kramer, from the third grade. Without these two, there probably would not have been a story.

John Stanislaw deserves credit for his keen-eyed and judicious editing. I'd also like to thank him for holding me back at times, when I went too far with some of my reflections.

Thanks to Jaime Salmonson for the photograph of the author that appears on the back cover.

I am particularly grateful to my friend, patient of thirty years, and *Newsday* sports editor Ed McNamara, who also helped in the editing. Ed's earnest encouragement, calling the material "great stuff, funny, and very deep in lots of places," helped push me to publish this book. He further reinforced this support by saying, "It has universal appeal to the millions of baby boomers who've been to or will be attending a fiftieth high school reunion." His emphatic statements definitely influenced the printing.

Ron Salmonson—sillysal@optonline.net

CONTENTS

BEFORE THE BEGINNING

Recently and somewhat reticently, I attended the highly anticipated fiftieth high school reunion at Midwood, a Brooklyn
school of four thousand students from which I never graduated.
Over a half century ago, I was expelled seven months before
graduation for committing larceny. I was one of five athletes tak-
en into custody for stealing gym equipment and other items. We
were thrown out and sent to different neighboring high schools
to complete our secondary educations. The degradation from the
incident—the arrest, mug shots, and fingerprinting—completely
crushed my world. I still remember trying to wash the black ink
off my finger tips, but I could not. It was like a tattoo—but the real
tattoo was forever embedded in my brain. The chapter of my life
called youth had now permanently closed. This series of events and
their ramifications shaped me in a lasting way. Understandably,
due to the stigma of my infamous history and never having attended a reunion, I was apprehensive as to whom I'd meet and how it
would go. I've read that life's best lessons are usually learned from
one's worst mistakes.

Pumped up for the event, I hunted for days and eventually found my dusty yearbook. Turning back the years in pages made me aware that I'm rapidly approaching my eighth decade. Every day I'm in quantum denial because the numbers of my life just don't match up with my inner-child mentality.

I waxed nostalgic as I looked back at those fading faces, which coincided with my washed-out memories of that long-ago past. Remarkably, I still see several guys from high school, but, unfortunately for all, we obviously don't remotely hold a candle to what we once looked like.

The celebratory event took place in lower Manhattan, chosen because some of us were present when Native Americans inhabited this area and watched Henry Hudson sail his *Half Moon* into New York's harbor. Midwood's alumni were now the ones having "reservations" at a convention center accommodating approximately two hundred guests. Upon arrival, I was shocked to see one or two assisted-living ambulettes dropping off their clients, who, by the way, were wearing the school colors, blue and white. My wife didn't attend because her fiftieth high school reunion was taking place the same night.

OUTSIDE THE BALLROOM

Prior to the 7:00 p.m. start, small groups of graduates hovered at various entrances, enthusiastically waiting for the event to begin. At the entry where I lingered, approximately twelve people sans spouses buzzed about, eyeballing one another. From their blank looks and questioning conversations, it was obvious not one recognized any of the others. This large Brooklyn school had a graduating class of way over a thousand. Moments later, an eye-catching, vivacious couple wandered over to our entrance doorway. I was immediately captivated by this younger-than-her-years woman, who had the most dazzling smile. I'm a dentist and notice exceptional pearly whites. As a matter of fact, her smile and bleachaholic white teeth resembled Farrah Fawcett in her heyday. I couldn't take my eyes off her.

This stunning woman's bubbly personality at once impressed the group. She revealed, "I'm Jeanne, maiden name Leventhal, lived on East Twenty-First and Avenue J. My husband and I flew in from Ohio for the week and are making a holiday of it."

Eyeing this attractive lady, I wondered if I was imagining this— or could her upper front tooth be getting longer? As I stared, I concluded it was! She turned to talk to someone, and when she turned back, her front tooth was gone! Faster than a speeding bullet, her hand rose to cover her mouth. In an instant, I realized what happened. All her teeth had been capped. Her front tooth snapped, totally amputating the underlying tooth structure that held the cap in place, right down to the gum line. The broken-off tooth was embedded inside her cap, which she held in the hand not covering her mouth.

Looking back, I surmised Jeanne's crown fractured off very recently. In the hope of getting the cap to stay on for the reunion, she purchased dental cement in a pharmacy. The tooth elongated as the adhesive gradually gave out. To say Jeanne was frantic was a gross understatement. Flabbergasted, her classmates gawked at her with their mouths agape.

After seemingly a never-ending time, my professional instincts took over, and I announced, to everyone's surprise, "I'm a dentist, and just maybe I could help." You wouldn't have believed this horror-stricken woman's reaction. First, her whole body seemed to relax, followed by the most preposterous missing-front-tooth smile you've probably never seen.

Jeanne then lisped awkwardly, "You mutht have been thent thraight from heaven." Now I must pause to confess, to me anyone missing a front tooth immediately loses forty IQ points.

All eyes were riveted on me as I asked for the crown. Even before taking it, I knew there was absolutely nothing any dentist could do without having access to a dental office. However, since everyone was staring at me, I didn't want to let her down.

Completely unglued and upset, she pleaded, "I'll do anything!"

Flailing at any possibility, I did finally have an epiphany and stated, "Actually, there's one thing you might do to get you through the reunion."

She begged again. "Whatever you say!"

Trying to hide my coy smile but, on the other hand, playing games with these unfamiliar faces, I paused for dramatic effect and asked, "Do you smoke?" For a second, no one in the group envisioned where I was going. Toothless Jeanne was the first to visualize the cigarette in her empty space and exploded with laughter. I thought about using my iPhone to take a picture but compassionately changed my mind. Jeanne's toothless laughter became infectious, as everyone watching Jeanne's comical laugh cracked up, which helped cut the palpable tension a bit. I'm sure everyone realized her uncontrollable laughter stemmed from the dichotomous emotional responses of being mortified and realizing how comedic she looked.

Finally, after the laughter died down and without batting an eye, I asked Jeanne, "By the way, do you have a dental insurance form?" This precipitated another round of side-splitting laughter, which coincided with the banquet hall opening, allowing the eager throngs of former students to rush in. For me, however, the open doors signaled, first and foremost, going back in time. By the way, I never saw the couple again and assumed they were looking for a dentist.

LET THE FESTIVITIES
COMMENCE

Although partially loosened from the missing-tooth incident, I immediately headed over to the bar and ordered a martini, hoping to chill out some more. Remember, I was kicked out of Midwood and didn't have a clue, fifty years later, whether they'd treat me as a pariah or give me a pardon.

I heard through the grapevine my criminal accomplice, basketball backcourt mate, and fellow jailbird Ken Slater would be attending. Unbelievably, a few alumni away, Ken, with wife at his elbow, were having a drink. Instantly, he called to me, "There's Baby!" I always loved the nickname because, besides announcing I was the youngest, it also passed the word that I made the grade with the older guys. To this day, I've kept this feeling of mental youthfulness, though I'm one of the oldest, I know. That night I loved the paradox of looking seventy juxtaposed with Kenny's taking me back to where we left off by calling me Baby. Besides making me smile because of its absurdity, it added to going back to the good old days.

Immediately, we gave each other a sincere hug, as fond friends who hadn't seen each other for ages often do, showing our mutual affection. Despite it being a half century since we last met, we resumed our closeness as if we had spoken yesterday! He looked great—fit and athletic, as if he had just stepped off the basketball hardwood.

"I wanna find out who your trainer is," I kidded.

Classmates who knew our history watched in disbelief as we caught up, disregarding everyone around. Nonetheless, there were more than a few schoolmates who not too discreetly pointed fingers at us, resurrecting the past feelings of shame and disgrace. One alumnus, who I had looked forward to seeing, playfully asked, "What are you guys talking about?"

Without batting an eye, I poker-faced, "Planning our next heist!"

Ken's lovely wife, who had been listening to our lengthy, animated conversation, revealed, "After forty years of marriage, I never knew a lot of this. Ken has always been very embarrassed by this episode. As a matter of fact, only recently did he tell our daughter about this. I've told him that some things in life can't be undone or forgotten. They change you forever. Never regret anything that's happened. Take it all as lessons learned, and move on with grace."

The reunited backcourt tandem pledged to get together with our wives in a quieter setting. Before mingling with the other Midwood grads, my accessory to the crime ironically shared, "I captained the University of Vermont's basketball team, got my PhD in psychology, and recently retired from a career in high school guidance."

As I walked away, two clichés popped into my mind: rekindled friendships can burn more brightly, and personal connections always mean more than the results on a scoreboard.

THE SETTING

Sauntering around the ballroom, I was now really into it as I hunted for familiar classmates. Looking closely at their faces, I tried to penetrate the ancient masks they wore, searching high and low for some clues that could wipe away a half century. I recognized some from their facial features, but more often than not, I had to stare at their name tags and high school pictures pinned to their chests. In contrast, when people looked for mine, I was anonymous because I didn't have one. I was expelled before the senior photos were taken. The preposterous idea of people thinking I crashed the event did cross my mind.

Because I had to extend my neck and slyly try to read virtually every name tag, I was not surprised that my neck became stiff and eyes strained from this rubbernecking.

Somewhat emboldened by my martini, I plunged into a crowd of unknowns and asked an attractive woman, who was schmoozing with friends, "Is that a picture of your granddaughter you're wearing?" To this day, I really don't understand why she split so abruptly, after this seemingly witty, flattering remark. This uncomfortable incident brought me back to my awkward adolescence, where every day I had episodes of embarrassment, or so it seemed.

Unfortunately, because it was difficult to see in this dimly lit room, a woman became anxious thinking I came too close, eyeballing her chest. Feeling distressed because of the lady's suspicions of my doing something inappropriate, I immediately felt my body's runaway perspiration switch into action. However, fortunately for me, I was wearing a sports coat, so I didn't have to sweat the problem, but I did run away.

In high school, almost on a daily basis, I was the butt of my classmates' jokes because I had underarm perspiration and foot-odor problems. Frequently, the rings under my armpits became so enormous the stains from one armpit would join the other. I remember getting tired thinking of ways of keeping my arms cemented to my sides. What's more, if I was invited to a party and knew in advance the kid's parents required the guests to take off their shoes, I wouldn't go.

With the clock approaching 8:00 p.m., famished, I scurried over to the buffet for food. However, unexpectedly, the line was at a standstill because two handicapped classmates, prisoners in their wheelchairs, were tangled up. These unfortunate people, who I'm sure were looking forward to the reunion after escaping from their assisted-living facilities, were visibly embarrassed. In the hubbub, thinking few were watching and fewer knew me, I saw my opportunity and bolted for the food.

PHYSICAL CHANGES

Searching for a quiet table, I found a corner seat, where a woman was eating alone. While inhaling my food, I looked around and studied my peers. It appeared a lot of old people were invited to my fiftieth. By the way, if you think things improve with age, go to a reunion.

Disturbingly, the men had changed more than I'd anticipated. They were noticeably smaller, gray, and had significantly reduced muscle mass. A handful shuffling about conjured up images of the Incredible Shrinking Man—stooped, stiff limbed, and certainly no longer al dente. Everyone here, like myself, once young and vital, was now growing small. Many were in various stages of balding. Their heads reminded me of the comedian Carrot Top's line about men's baldness: "At least it shows God has a sense of humor." Not surprisingly, a lot of men had more hair on their faces than heads. I also didn't anticipate the number wearing hearing aids. I'm sensitized to hearing loss; hereditarily, I'm following my dad, who was afflicted. Dentistry's high-pitched, ear-splitting drills also factor in.

While reflecting on hearing aids, I noticed an old buddy, Paul Horen, wearing one. As I said hello, it was obvious from his dazed look that Paul had no idea who I was. I thought maybe he didn't recognize me because I had changed so much. Then I presumed perhaps he couldn't hear, or maybe he was losing it. I also considered it could've been a combination of all three.

Straining to hear, Horen came uncomfortably close, invading my space as many hearing-impaired people do, and bellowed, "What ya say?" After I repeated my name at full volume, Paul successfully rolled back the years and smiled. Pointing to his hearing aids, he said, "These fuckin' things barely work, though they did come in handy last week at my grandson's bar mitzvah. I turned them off while the DJ played Smashing Pumpkins or whatever music it was that wakes the dead."

After a few minutes of us chitchatting, the years peeled away, and we pretty much reverted to where we left off as teens. Candidly, I revealed, "At times I struggle to hear, and I'm wondering if I should try hearing aids."

Without batting an eye, Paul took his hearing aids out and said, "Here, give them a try."

Placing them in, I almost staggered from the strident, high-pitched static. After regaining my equilibrium, I sashayed away from Paul—his eyes remaining riveted on me, I'm sure—and searched for a classmate to play with. Fred Lauschen, my sidekick from junior high, was the lucky cohort I chose to kibitz with. After putting my right ear and then left exaggeratedly in his face, Freddy noticed the hearing aids. Grinning ear to ear, Fred said in a normal voice, "I can tell you're hearing better."

I replied (very loudly, of course), "What ya say…what ya say… what?" Now I could more easily understand why some hearing impaired, even with hearing aids, could be deaf to others.

After returning Paul's hearing aids and watching him walk away, I noticed he and a decent number of alumni, myself included, displayed that round-shouldered, stooped, hunchback posture. From time to time, I've wondered, is this an evolutionary change? Starting at forty, both sexes lose about half an inch in height per decade. This occurs because the disks between our vertebrae become dry and thin. With this loss of stature and humpbacked curvature, maybe it's nature's way of combatting the loss of balance and decreased vision often associated with aging. Is this a transformative effect? By making man closer to the ground, is nature trying to minimize people breaking bones from falling? However, isn't it ironic that with age you get shorter, yet when you bend to pick up something, doesn't the ground seem farther away than it used to be?

Today, health professionals warn of a new medical condition called "text neck" or "tech neck." This is a curvature of the neck resulting from the overuse of handheld technological devices or texting. I believe their usage, presently more prevalent in young people, will exacerbate future generations' aforementioned forward and downward neck curvatures. Together, these two phenomena will cause more neck, spinal, and future medical problems. These difficulties will become more magnified and damaging as man's longevity increases. Since I have text neck already without texting, I wonder if I fool a few people that I'm more technologically sophisticated than in actuality.

The women, spruced up by their makeup, dyed hair, facelifts, cosmetic dentistry, and Sunday-best attire, fared much better, though surprisingly they lost more height than men. Deep in thought, I was unexpectedly taken by surprise upon seeing two familiar women approaching.

THE JANE GIRLS

It was the Jane girls, Jane Bates and Plain Jane Jaffe. Jane Bates, dressed up to the nines, just as at Midwood, had lived a few blocks away in a large Victorian house. I often heard about Jane and her little brother because our mothers were friends from grade school. In high school, Bates was voted Best Dressed, and that night she could've won that distinction again. As a teen everything about her had incomparable style. She could've worn anything with the same bearing. Back then, her tall figure was striking, an eye-catching combination of sophistication and grace. Fifty years later, Bates looked a lot like her mother, with the same frosted hair—and she even had grown hips like her, too!

Ms. Bates was with Jane Jaffe, a.k.a. Plain Jane, her conjoined-at-the-hip friend since junior high. Long ago, behind Jane Jaffe's back, someone nicknamed her Plain Jane because she was a quiet, homely, stripped-down version of her bedecked sidekick, Jane Bates. However, that night, bosom buddy Plain Jane was not so plain! This evening she dressed up in a red outfit, which clung to her body in all the right places. Plain Jane personified Lady

Duff-Gordon's line, "Put the plainest woman in a beautiful dress, and unconsciously she'll give her best shot to live up to it."

"Hello, Jane Bates! Someone mentioned you've remarried, but I don't have a clue what your new name is. Love your outfit and hair. You certainly look great; never saw you so thin. Don't hear a whole lot about you since our moms died," I remarked.

"Don't bother with the name. You'll like this one. Might've gotten remarried to get out of Brooklyn and get a new name and a *dress!* I split with my husband after a few years. Bates it is again. Thanks for noticing; love the compliments. How are things going with you and Iris? I can't believe how many single people are here tonight," she responded.

"Iris and I are well. Still doing interior decorating?" I asked. Jane Bates was always into gussying things up, whether it was herself, houses, or whatever. As a kid she had a natural flair for design, and I heard she did exceptionally well in business.

"Yeah, still doing it, but less. Surprisingly, I'm a lot less into clothes these days. Don't have the energy to shop, try them on, and the bother of returning things. Maybe it's the age, but I still try to look sharp," she said.

Without doubt I still appreciate a woman who's into her outfits and style. But as I listened to Jane Bates, I couldn't help but picture the paradoxical other side of the coin. Many people love to spend money buying clothes, but never realize that some of the best moments in life are enjoyed without having any clothes on!

As Jane and I chatted, catching up with our lives, I couldn't help but wonder if my own clothes were suitable for the night, especially in front of this lady of haute couture. Since I was never into shopping, my philosophy has been to just wear clothes that fit in. I don't want to be outstanding in the sense people point at me and say, "Do you believe what he's wearing? Did he look in the mirror?" While Jane Bates talked, my mind segued to my favorite quote regarding embellishments, one I saw in Mark Twain's living room in Hartford, Connecticut: "The decorations of my house are adorned with the friends who frequent it." Absolutely love it! While on the subject, I'd like to give my advanced-years peer group a new fashion guideline that's age appropriate. I'll call it Ron's Rule—the more you cover yourself up, the better you'll look.

Let me digress for a moment. I must tell you, every time I watch *Downton Abbey* on TV, I think of Brooklyn's Jane Bates because there's an English couple on the show with the same surname, Bates. This TV couple is having their first child, which they state will be a boy. When I was about nine, Midwood's Jane Bates's much-younger brother was born. Since that time, I've always called her little brother Master Bates. Considering this might be the last time I see Jane, should I tell her that sometimes when I think about her, "Master Bates" enters my thoughts?

PERCEPTIONS

Feeling better after having eaten and experiencing a buzz from my libations, I returned to the far corner table where that lone woman sat, discovering she'd been joined by four gray people. Listening to their rather uninteresting conversations, I learned they were all husbands or wives of classmates. All pretty much miserable, commiserating about the never-ending, boring night, these not-part-of-the-action spouses became the target recipients of my latest reflection. I said, "I know when you look around, you're thinking this place is packed with ancient people."

Immediately, the woman I had met earlier smirked. I believed she was on the same page as I, which she confirmed by confessing, "Just look what the ravages of time did to the people here tonight. Most of them look like they should be in Florida, or, as they call it, God's waiting room."

Responding to her viewpoint, I countered, "Truth be told, I don't think they see themselves as being antiquated. They're not young and vibrant like they were in Midwood, but see themselves as older folks we used to see but never thought we'd become.

16

Nevertheless, the alumni here tonight look at each other as teenagers, when fun and games were the way of life. They played their forty-fives and had few responsibilities. Stick around; I think everyone will loosen up as the night unfolds." Being a stranger to every spouse at the table and also an outsider to many of the alumni because I never graduated, I excused myself, pretending I had a call from nature.

Taking a break, I walked out into the hallway, found a cozy couch, called time out, and got lost in thought, thinking of the good old days. Back then my perception of Midwood's students was that you were either a jock or a nonjock. I suppose if you really wanted to complicate things, you could divide the nonjock category into four categories: the Brains, the Prom Queens, the Hoods, and the endless nameless, simply known as the Invisible People. Most fitting this latter category were of course nonexistent at the reunion. A few of the Hoods did show. Not surprisingly, many of the Hoods reported taking up law enforcement as a career. I guess they were used to dealing with the law, being a little crooked, or as bullies they gravitated toward positions of power.

Looking back, similar to most metropolitan areas, my Brooklyn school was comprised of various races, religions, and nationalities, a typical melting pot. Each group had its unique differences, which were embraced and celebrated. These dissimilarities helped us learn from each other. I suppose because we were all a little different, this made us more similar than we imagined.

CIRCULATING THE BALLROOM

R ealizing time was fleeting, I traipsed back inside and scoured the room for more familiar faces. Walking around, I encountered many people gathered in their own little parties. Purposely eavesdropping, I discovered a significant percentage of my colleagues were independent, quite active, and contributing to society. The same factors predicting happiness among younger people apply to this age, including good health, friends, and financial security. Many had updated their skills through lifelong learning.

Some talked of travel, a number volunteered, and, somewhat surprising, quite a few had second careers. As expected, the most consistent theme was enjoying more time with family. Not unpredictably, several mentioned religion becoming more important with age. Other interesting comments included one from a smiling contemporary who said, "You're never too old to feel young." Louise, an obviously perceptive woman, stated, "I rarely feel age. If you have creative work, whether it's the arts, writing, or activities worth doing, there's not enough time. You're passionate and don't have a minute to become old." A thought from an unknown

Invisible Person I related to well summed it up best: "Just as I begin to feel I could make good use of time, there's so little time left. That's a quote I read somewhere."

When people realize the hands of time keeps ticking at their backs and their days are becoming numbered, I get the impression their priorities begin to shift. Older individuals, for sure, seem more present oriented than younger people and more selective with whom they spend time. They also seem more forgiving and care more for others and less about enhancing themselves.

Nevertheless, a significant number of conversations dwelled on who's gained the most weight, who's successful, who's still married and to whom, and who's lost the most hair. I guess the priorities of these classmates got lost along the way. For this group, it was basically a beauty pageant, if they didn't kid themselves. However, for most, fortunately, it wasn't about who you were then but who you are now.

TARNISHED ELEGANCE

U nexpectedly, I thought I saw Susan Sorrento or someone who reminded me of her. In high school, she was every schoolgirl's worst nightmare. You know the type. Besides being voted the prettiest, she had a knockout body and matching personality. Preposterously, Susan was elected president of the scholastic society, and, to further ice the cake, her athleticism was showcased on the tennis court, where she played first singles. Thinking back, I'm sure this masterpiece was the muse of a lot of wet dreams of the guys I hung out with.

These attributes enhanced her gracefulness on the dance floor. It requires athleticism to dance, but she was also an artist on the dance floor. Susan was a stunning superstar, physically gorgeous, and a goddess in motion. She owned every single room she entered. How often does anyone simultaneously have these exceptional attributes? We're talking on the level of a Ginger Rogers (dancing partner of the legendary Fred Astaire). Once in a blue moon, the genetic lottery hits a grand slam! As a teenager, Susan should've been ashamed of the things she could do to adolescent boys or men. Unbelievably, though, these gifts never went to her head. For this writer, her only possible imperfection was that she had no flaws. As you can tell, every guy worshipped her from afar. But do you think I did?

I'll always remember how Susan danced with the spectacular Howie King, voted the best male dancer in this large Brooklyn school. Circles formed around them, jaws dropped as we watched in awe as the two rock-and-rolled. He was great, but Susan might've been better, as someone pointed out; she did everything as well, but did it backward, following his lead, and sometimes in high-heeled shoes.

She was so far out of my league, it would've been absolutely useless for me to try, but how could I not fantasize? I had my share of self-doubts and lack of confidence. I was not a Prince Charming nor remotely attractive. I was frightfully thin and dealt poorly with the ravages of acne. Additionally, having skipped a grade, I was younger than just about everyone in our class. This was packaged with no car or money. These shortcomings helped me come in last in receiving valentines (though I did have a few imaginary ones). My forte was providing vicarious "lines" to brainy jocks who tried to date Midwood's upper-echelon beauties. I read in some romance story, probably Archie comics, "All really great lovers are articulate, and verbal seduction is the surest road to actual seduction" (M. Mannes). These observations confirmed my limited experience when it came to affairs of the heart: a man is inclined to fall in love through his eyes, a woman through her ears.

It is now easy to understand why I was so upset to see how the geometry of Susan's figure had changed. Go figure, this former absolute goddess had gained at least seventy pounds, and as I watched her struggle to get out of a chair, I noticed she'd long ago lost her leggy, foal-like charms. In addition, her knockout smile, which she used as a weapon in high school, was now a nightmare. Besides missing some teeth, the remaining were periodontally elongated, similar to Bugs Bunny. Everything about her arms, shoulders, neck, and face had ballooned. She looked like a chubby grand-mother who worked a checkout in Walmart. I wondered, "Are the other women as shaken as I am?"

"Time is the great equalizer. It is a cruel thief that robs us of our former selves. We lose as much to life as we do to death" (E. F. Hailey). Another double-edged saying, "Aging is the only way to live a long life," gives a different perspective.

I recall as kids, we acted as if we were the first young people who ever inhabited this world. With age, you become totally aware that what has happened to you has occurred to everyone from the beginning of time. Some alumni found satisfying ironies; the cap-tain of the football team had replacement knees and a beer belly and was thrice divorced. Other former athletes leaned on canes, while onetime cheerleaders now were frumpy senior citizens. The brainiest kid in our class, who received a PhD in nuclear astrophys-ics, dropped out of academia to raise llamas.

I can understand why some classmates didn't come to the reunion. Today it's somewhat less exciting reconnecting with fellow graduates because of Facebook or other social media ave-nues. Before the Internet, previous generations could not follow each other (although, as they say, you can't hug someone on the Internet). This accessibility could backfire, as my friend Sy said: "I saw my old flame on Facebook. She looked like an orangutan! Don't wanna see her." Some alumni didn't make the scene, I was told, because they were too ashamed of their current situations; others paradoxically were too snobby because of their success.

A few classmates prepared for the reunion months in advance. I overheard one woman who I did remember say, "I had a face-lift, dyed my hair, spent a ton of time at the gym, and lost eighty pounds." Her friend rejoined, "I lost forty pounds by becoming a vegetarian." Looking at the second lady, whom I didn't recognize at all, I thought, "Don't ever remember seeing *herbivore.*" A third woman, whom I remembered as being funny in school, gave these snappy quips: "I try to avoid things that make me feel fat—like mirrors, photographs, and scales. I also wish I weighed what I weighed when I first thought I was fat." Another lady restated an old-as-the-hills line: "I don't want to make anyone jealous, but I still fit into the same earrings I wore at Midwood." Overall, the women's appearances ranged from relatively youthful womanhood to elderly haghood. Surprisingly, a few eye-catching women changed for the better. I'm sure the other women hated them. This contrasted to an equal number who looked assisted-living ready.

DO I LOOK AS OLD AS HIM?

One of the endlessly fascinating and frustrating aspects of our pictorial life history is how little control we have over the way we age, the way others see us, and how we see ourselves. Looking back, we're well aware how in different times of life, we change physically. Some kids are gorgeous as babies, even favorably compared to the well-remembered Gerber baby. Other babies, as noted on *Seinfeld*, are downright ugly. Some youngsters, stunning in elementary school, lose their adorableness passing through puberty. At various stages, change can take the same individual from being attractive to being a turnoff. A minority of women become more beautiful with age, while some men in time resemble Popeye.

One guy who never married said, "When I was a kid, I was the ugliest kid in the class. Alfred E. Neuman from *Mad* magazine made me look good. The so-called cool guys used me as the butt of their jokes. I never had any self-esteem or confidence and painfully shied away from girls. Today I'm lucky, because I have this full crop of hair and spend some time in the gym; women swarm after me. Nevertheless, to this day, the insecurities I acquired in childhood pervade my consciousness. The early years are critical in formulating your personality."

Incredulously, though my classmates' looks and bodies were wearing away in tandem, nearly all of their personalities were there, just below the surface. It knocks me for a loop; nowadays my mind can't believe what my body looks like. Over time, the way you perceive yourself and the way you're seen drift further and further apart. When I was a kid, my mother would repeatedly say, "It happened so fast!" As much as I disagreed with her on so many things, she was absolutely correct. It seems like I was young only a moment ago. On the Internet, I've read seniors feel thirteen years younger than their age. Accordingly, I love to ask my peers, "How old do you feel mentally?" The quote "Inside every older person is a young person wondering what the hell happened" is right on!

Humans develop by accumulating layers. Adults are really kids with multiple layers. I've only been part of my classmates' early stages and believe most people don't change. Fundamentally we stay the same, even with success or failure, which merely amplifies what's already there. Because our body changes and we generally don't, it causes great confusion. All old people share this secret. As I made my way around the ballroom, I could identify a few individuals by their faces or eyes. Others, it was their telltale voices, smiles, or gaits. The majority, however, I couldn't place at all.

On the other hand, with a few classmates, my brain searched, trying to remember what was so familiar. Finally, in time, I had an epiphany—it was him! This person, who was looking at me, was thinking the same thing. Jubilation occurs only after sifting through lots of layers. We had discovered an ancestral friend! Instantaneously, we were yapping away as though we had spoken recently. Be that as it may, the two of us, in the backs of our minds, were thinking, "How did he get so old? Do I look as bad as him?"

Underneath the various strata, most alumni shared the basic foundation of growing up in Flatbush. However, each classmate acquired different layers through the course of his or her personalized journey. Of course, the more coats you accumulate, the harder it becomes to see the underlying real you. Nevertheless, similar to wearing layered winter clothing, it was amazing how quickly most peeled off their outer garments and reverted to their earlier years. Awesome! Once they did, the telltale signs of their youth reemerged, and watching them spirit about was phenomenal. Nothing makes you feel younger than being with those who knew you when you were actually young. It was an event where essentially everyone showed up old and grew younger as the night went on. We all acted like kids; the fiftieth turned into a reunion of teenage senior citizens!

Juxtaposing the euphoria of seeing forgotten classmates, waves of foreboding crept into my mind as I changed the rhythms of my musings. During this absolute blast, murky thoughts of inescapable future battles plagued my brain. An underlying hidden mask of concern and fear most certainly lay ahead. "How many layers do I have left?" I wondered. As we enter our seventies, every day seems a little faster as we watch time gallop away. Sometimes I feel like every twenty minutes I'm eating breakfast. This peer group will surely have to face unspoken tragedies, whether they'll be the inevitable health issues or loved ones passing.

How frequently has a last time come (people and things), and we're not conscious of it? I'm constantly aware that my tomorrows are numbered and time is dwindling. People come and go in life. You must never miss the opportunity to tell these prized individuals how much they mean to you. "Death is a debt we all must pay; for the gift of life which we have to repay" (Euripides). "The more sand escapes from the hourglass of our life, the clearer we should be able to see" (H. L. Mencken). Clearly, I don't like what I see. But by putting these thoughts on paper, maybe it'll allow me to live a little longer after I'm gone.

RECONNECTING WITH
FORMER FRIENDS

While brooding in self-contemplation, I lost count of the many mini hot dogs I ate. Fortunately for my digestive tract, pants size, and depressive thoughts, I was startled out of my reverie by a hard slap to the back of my head, strong enough to make me wince.

Quickly turning, I recognized the face of Barry Brill. Barry was nicknamed BB to his face, Psycho behind his back. Psycho roared, "I see you're not dead yet, but almost." At one time we were close. We first hooked up in Hebrew school, played ball together, and both skipped a grade in junior high. We also had our bar mitzvahs on the same day. In our early teens, BB was the wildest and weirdest of our many crazy friends. As a matter of fact, Psycho was voted the kid most likely to be the first one dead! He got into drugs before anyone had any idea what they were, had three kids, and divorced twice, all before the age of twenty. He tried everything in life except living. Growing up, BB lived in the huge Vandeveer housing project, which was also a mecca for NYC basketball. Every local basketball aficionado knew this was the place to play. Two NBA basketball players, Billy Cunningham and Doug Moe, had spent a lot of time bouncing the ball there.

BB invited me to Vandeveer, knowing I was a basketball freak with a reputation of being more than decent. The first time, in late spring on an exceptionally hot day, I was chomping at the bit and couldn't wait to play. I came early, rang his downstairs bell, and waited outside his tenement as Barry got ready. Due to the jungle heat, Barry's entire six-story building's windows were wide open. This was before air conditioning. BB finally came out and said, "Did you hear the music from the third floor?"

I said, "Yeah, what's the big deal? Someone's blasting the radio."

Barry said, "No, no, that's my neighbor Barbra singing. She's a couple of years older than us."

"No way," I said. "Really?"

Later at the schoolyard, Psycho pointed to a scrawny teen and said, "The girl you heard singing before—that's her over there." I stopped thumping the ball and gave her a double look because I couldn't believe any human could sing so well. I stared at this short, pony-tailed, big-nosed, homely looking girl playing with her friends. It was Barbra Streisand. After that, I went back to Barry's apartment house many times and got to know Barbra a little but couldn't tolerate her. She was brash, arrogant, and too cocksure of herself. Not dating material! I'm sure she's still sorry.

One Saturday, Barry beckoned me to play hoops with him again. Unfortunately, at 10:00 a.m., all seventeen courts were taken except for one, where four old guys were shooting around. The adults, in their midforties, out-aged us by thirty years. These old men were physically imposing and used their weight to slow down their spry, skinny opponents. We played half court, three on three, with the winning team staying to play the next threesome. One elderly, heavy guy was playing BB exceptionally rough, holding him or his shirt, banging him, and the like. Psycho couldn't take it, went ballistic, and literally had a fistfight with the old geezer. BB was absolutely no match for this over-two-hundred-pound guy. From a barrage of blows, Barry got pummeled and had to stop playing.

Needless to say, I left with him and attempted to make him feel better, saying, "How could you possibly fight him? He outweighed you by sixty pounds and was six inches taller."

After a few seconds, I saw tears rolling down Barry's cheeks. He then said haltingly, "The guy I fought was my father, the bastard! We don't get along. I guess you could tell—a very sad situation."

"Are you shitting me? No way!" I blurted.

"Yeah, I didn't want to tell ya before we played." He whimpered, struggling to get his words out. He throbbed physically, of course, but the emotional assault to his ego was the bigger hurt. With his newly grown fat lip, BB now lisped, which paradoxically made the scene somewhat comical. To this day I've never seen a father and son have a fistfight, let alone on a basketball court!

Winding down our conversation at the reunion, Barry proudly shared, "I turned my life around after major battles with drugs and alcohol. I picked up a graduate degree from Columbia in psycho-therapy, am happily married to my fourth wife, and live in Raleigh, North Carolina, treating drug and sex addicts."

After chatting awhile longer, I told the transformed Psycho, "Time is flying. There are so many people I want to see. Don't be offended, but I've got to cut ya short."

Barry responded, "I totally understand. I'll be doing the same. By the way, don't spend any more time in jail."

FORMER TEAMMATES AND EX-JOCKS

S trolling over to a nearby table, I grabbed the last available chair, where a number of ex-jocks in varying states of decline were shooting the breeze. About five of the has-beens were in the midst of rehashing some big game as if it occurred yesterday. High school stars are forever living in the past, as if no part of their lives, before or after, was as real as the years they played the game. Don't get me wrong, we all try to hold on to good things from the past, but for these guys, it was almost as if they knew it would never get any better than the moments they shared competing in the various arenas.

I easily recognized all the basketball players but only a few footballers. In high school, I consciously stayed away from these gridironers because they were the same guys who in elementary school beat the crap out of you for no legitimate reason. In spite of my deliberate avoidance of football players, they seemed to remember this infamous guy more than I recalled them. At

Midwood, fueled by their raging testosterone levels, they were rewarded for their belligerent behavior by playing football. Louie Heil, an obnoxious, quintessential bully even as a kid, was there. I knew him well because he lived a block away. As a kid Louie was a nasty tyke who was hard to like, who ultimately mushroomed into a three-hundred-pound defensive tackle everyone avoided like the plague. He had a face that looked like he washed it every day with steel wool. His sarcastic street talk always had a serrated bite to it, which incidentally was a pretty good way of describing lots of guys I grew up with.

Therefore, I wasn't totally surprised that after Louie said hello, he smirked and bellowed, "I was hoping you'd show your face. Do you still have any of those football jerseys you stole from Midwood?"

Later that night, one of Louie's teammates told me, "I heard Louie went into his father's demolition business and was doing well." Certainly appropriate! I thought. There he could find some measure of satisfaction by still harboring his affinity for destruction.

Flamboyant Marty Krauss, affectionately buddy-buddy with another guy, slowly strutted past our table, catching the eye of Louie. Repugnant Heil, still the tormenter, stood up and at full volume burst out with, "Look who's here, guys, it's Mary Kraus."

Back then, we knew Marty was different. A dainty, effeminate teen, he was kind of blatant about his sexual orientation. Fifty years ago, most gays—maybe he was transgender—weren't comfortable coming out of the closet. In high school, maverick Marty even flaunted his sexual preference when he enrolled in ballet school, where he was the only male in the class. At that time in Brooklyn, it was unheard of for a guy to be taking toe dancing.

After one class, a girl reported to her football-playing boyfriend, "Marty got kicked out of ballet class because he injured a groin muscle."

The perplexed boyfriend asked, "That's strange; why would they kick him out for that?" The girlfriend answered, "It wasn't his groin muscle."

This dance class story reminded me of a joke George Carlin did on TV: "I knew a transsexual guy whose only ambition was to eat, drink, and be Mary." And of course, after Louie Heil heard about the pubic area incident, he transgendered Marty's name to Mary; henceforth Kraus's name was changed forever.

It was enjoyable seeing my fellow cager Band-Aid Barry Fisher holding court at the jock table. Barry got his moniker from always being hurt, tripping, and banging into things. Therefore, many of us were not completely surprised when he showed up at the reunion with a cast. Just as many people weren't surprised that he'd become an orthopedic surgeon too. Ironically, Barry sat next to Marty Doctors—no misprint—a center on our basketball team who also became a physician. I guess one could say tongue in cheek that they were a paradox. (Pair of docs—or was it three docs? Dr. Fisher and Dr. Doctors.)

In high school, Marty Doctors, six foot eight, was rather introverted. He almost seemed reclusive, which was difficult because of his gigantic size. Keeping with his backdoor bashfulness, Doctors went into proctology, which treats rectums and anuses. (Has anyone ever seen the plural of "anus"? But I'm sure we've all seen a whole lot of assholes in our lives.)

Though dentists know the mouth is the dirtiest place in the body, I could never understand why a physician would desire to earn a living servicing this other orifice. After learning Doctors became a proctologist and knowing that Marty Doctors's parents, the Doctorses, spoke Yiddish, I couldn't help but think his parents would smile if they heard the scatological nickname I gave their son: the Farkakta Doctor—Dr. Doctors.

In hindsight, I wonder if Dr. Doctors's career choice was influenced by his interest in humor and/or affinity for vanity license plates. "ASS MD" could've been a great choice, but Marty was much too reserved and inhibited for that, so that wasn't an option. "TUSH MD," a softer version and good first choice, would've caught my eye if I drove behind him.

A second option (I have had a special fondness for initials since childhood—more on that later) was MD MD (Martin Doctors—Medical Doctor). This could've been a doubly venerated choice. Personally, I think I would've gone for number two, even though I liked number one a lot.

Seated at the jock table on my other side was Sam Bealeau (pronounced "below") a former close friend, who couldn't come close to making the squad but ended up managing our team. Sam loved the game but rarely was called when choosing sides for basketball. "Hello, Bealeau, what's up?" I inquired with a smile. This play on words, which I started before junior high, always made us revert back to thinking of ourselves as juveniles.

"Not much, just a lifetime gone by."

During our conversation, I learned Bealeau had retired from a career in finance and recently purchased a home just below Boca Raton. My interest piqued, I found it extremely thought provoking that this money man almost immediately started talking about his personal struggles, removing money from his retirement accounts, and the like.

Nodding, I said, "I know exactly where you're coming from. You're the first person I've heard who's put those thoughts into words. I don't think I'll ever get used to watching my nest egg siphoned off for retirement, either."

Sam said, "A good chunk of your financial life is built around saving for retirement. Now that I'm done working, I find it very difficult withdrawing from my retirement accounts. After all these years, it's not easy to retrain yourself. I get agitated and feel guilty every time I take out money. Because my mind-set has been so entrenched in saving, I can't imagine ever getting used to it. On the other hand, since today's retirees are living longer, they'll likely spend more years not working than previous generations. Therefore, it's important we paradoxically save, trying to ensure we'll still have enough money for our later years."

All the ex-jocks' conversations came to an abrupt halt when a list being passed around landed in the hands of Midwood's ex-quarterback, Mel Evans. As an aside, I heard this onetime Adonis wasn't doing well, forgetting or "losing it," according to the source. I raised an eyebrow, thinking about the irony of the situation. In the old (young) days, one of Mel's strengths was his ability to forget a botched play he had just called, think positively, and move on. Now, on the other hand, "forgetting" had a foreboding, cruel, unspeakable meaning to many of those in attendance—the beginnings of cognitive impairment. Looking at the list, Mel put on his glasses and fumbled for a while before finally saying, "I can't read this. I forgot to bring my new reading glasses. Could someone read this for me?"

A geeky Greek basketball benchwarmer, Dimitris Spiliotis, whom we called Dummy behind his back, volunteered to read the list. After shaking his head a few times, Spiliotis insensitively commented, "This is a list of obituaries from our class. It's huge; you won't believe some of the names. I bet you've been dying to hear this." Almost every jock at the table cringed, either from the inappropriateness of the attempted pun or from recognizing the names of classmates that've passed.

I was blown away upon hearing the names of so many past friends vanished and gone and asked, "Did Midwood have more than most?"

Dimitris, nerdy as ever, stated, "Twenty-one percent of the males and thirteen percent of females is the national average. I looked it up on the Internet." We were all shocked by the high percentages.

"Is Killer Kramer on it? I'm surprised I haven't seen him here tonight," some guy asked.

KILLER KRAMER

Michael Kramer, from third grade to this day, has been one of my closest friends. Back then, finding friends with similar mental disorders was easy because, for the most part, everyone seemed nuts. "Part of being sane is to be a little crazy" (Janet Long). Going with the flow, I learned early in elementary school that in order to survive and function, you had to conceal this craziness beneath a thick blanket of conventional behavior. Even now I gravitate to people who are screwed up in some way or another—like myself, for example.

Michael is one of the guys I think of whenever I see or read something funny or something that makes me think. There are certain people I share things with. For instance, I'll e-mail a close friend and say, "You've got to read this; you're going to fall off your chair." To this day, I can think out loud in front of Michael, as good friends allow you to. He's always been there for meaningful conversations and advice. He'll also make time if you need him. Kramer, a true friend, is a person who makes your problems his problems.

His moniker was derived from Kramer almost killing our assistant principal, Klatsky.

Kramer and I, two of the bigger guys in class, were selected as book monitors. At the end of the year, we had the responsibility of returning hundreds of heavy textbooks to a subterranean stockroom. Very few students knew of, let alone were authorized to set foot into, this zigzagging, off-limits area. Furthermore, this basement locale housed a number of administrative offices that chronicled every student's grades, rank, and so on. Klatsky's office was down there.

After we stored the books, Kramer would run and hide, then jump out and startle me. On a particular day, Kramer stealthily ran ahead and hid as usual. Unexpectedly, I caught a glimpse of him disappearing behind an alcove. As I approached the assistant principal's office, Klatsky quietly came out. He was totally engrossed in reading a report while walking thirty feet ahead of me. Silently I cracked up, envisioning Kramer suddenly jumping out and scaring the shit out of the principal.

As I watched the comedic scene unfold, it played out perfectly— even might've won an Academy Award except, regrettably, it went haywire. In what seemed like slow motion, as Kramer leaped out, Klatsky staggered, grabbed his chest, dropped his papers, and collapsed to the ground, out cold! Michael and I looked at each other and were sure Klatsky was a goner! We then held our first medical conference, deciding Kramer would stay with Mr. K. while I sprinted two flights of stairs to the school nurse, who'd call an ambulance (before 9-1-1). The end results were that Klatsky had a mild heart attack but thankfully recovered, we lost our book jobs, and Michael was forever known as "Killer Kramer."

Getting back to the ex-jock's question, I answered, "Without doubt Kramer's alive, but I'm not sure why he didn't come. Ironically, he lives close enough to have almost walked here."

THE GIRL I SAT NEXT TO

While bidding adieu, I got up from my chair and, with a smile, informed the jocks, "I gotta run, but don't remember how." However, without a warning, with my first step I literally collided with a woman, almost causing her to keel over, à la Klatsky. "I'm so sorry; I wasn't paying attention. You OK?" I flustered. As I tried to regain my composure, my heart skipped a beat, zeroing in on this attractive lady. I was now doubly embarrassed: one, because of my clumsiness, and two, because, though she looked awfully familiar, I couldn't immediately come up with her name. Then all at once everything clicked: Laura Salmon. Blissfully, I was thrilled to see her in many ways.

Shaken by the collision, excitement of the night, or whatever, my heart suddenly began pounding away. I remember thinking, heart attack, heart attack! Acknowledging all this, I was a little less worried than you might've expected, because earlier in the night a classmate had asked me, "Have you caught up with Laura Salmon? Did you know she became a cardiologist?"

I didn't rush to tell Dr. Salmon about my problem because, thankfully, the palpitations subsided as fast as they started—this, coupled with Laura immediately asking, "How've you been? Tell me all about yourself."

Not being in the mood to talk, let alone about myself, I bided some time, making sure I was all right. While stalling, my favorite Native American saying came to mind: "Your tongue makes you deaf." I then seamlessly proceeded to turn the tables on her, asking about her life rather than discussing mine.

Admirably, upon recalling self-effacing Laura, I was not surprised when she played down her accomplishments, chronicling her formidable education, training, and the fact she still taught at a university hospital. Barely glossing over her personal life, she said, "I'm single, though I was married for ten years and have a son. I'm glad I kept my maiden name."

Unfortunately for me, after five minutes, a number of Laura's high school friends came by, interrupting our conversation. With a heavy heart, I waved good-bye, saying, "We must get together some time," knowing it would probably never happen—unless later that night my heart acted up, God forbid, and I needed treatment.

As I walked away, I reflected how it certainly was terrific seeing Laura. She looked great, better than she did as a teenager, and unpretentious as ever. Too bad she was single. I wonder if she had her son after divorcing her husband. That would make him a Salmonson. Smiling to myself, I thought, "Got to tell that to my sons." I've also got to tell them about the classic she pulled off when Delaney cards first came out.

Laura Salmon sat next to me in a couple of science and math classes. In those days, NYC high school instructors gave blank Delaney cards the first day of school, so teachers could locate where their students sat. If you know what a Delaney card is, you probably grew up in New York. Each student entered their name on these cards and the teacher filed them in a seating chart so it would be easy to identify the students. One first day of school, Laura surprisingly took an extra card and fictitiously wrote the name Dick Hertz on it. She was hoping to get a rise out of an unsuspecting neophyte female teacher. She also hoped to get the boys in hot water because the teacher never would've suspected a girl of pulling this stunt off. Of course, when the young lady teacher inquired, "Who's Dick Hertz?" Immediately, three or four guys frenziedly waved their hands, while they writhed and moaned raucously. Spontaneous, wild, booming laughter erupted from the class, rolling in waves, the kind of howling one almost never hears. When the class seemed like they didn't have another gasp left in them, and their weary ribs could stand no more, it would begin again, roaring and reverberating with renewed force, deafening the classroom over and over. The new, innocent teacher, conscious of what now had transpired, reddened, realizing the joke. She then turned a dark crimson after recognizing the joke was on her.

As far back as I can remember, Laura possessed sparkling, mischievous eyes, which went well with her playful smile and infectious laugh. She was brilliant, an Ivy League grad, and had a great personality and matching sense of humor. Ironically, she was a *belle laide*, an attractive woman despite not being conventionally beautiful. Incomprehensibly, in high school she was often shy and stayed to herself, despite the anomalous "Dick Hertz" incident. In later years she blossomed. She was one of those women who became more beautiful as she left her youth behind. Because Laura almost singlehandedly organized this reunion, she was honored to deliver the opening address.

Her keynote speech began, "As you know, our school colors were blue and white, and that's the reason I chose this white dress with blue accessories." The dress was sleeveless, very low cut, and showed her ample cleavage (which I don't remember and would have). Laura continued, "As you can see, I bought this dress specifically for this occasion. The dress was on sale...half off." Next, she looked down at her sexy dress and slowly pirouetted. She then glanced at her cleavage, gave the dress a tug at the top, and, with an infectious laugh, said suggestively, "And it's still half off!" Every person in the room, even the waiters and waitresses, roared with laughter. After Laura's superb introduction, the disc jockey played his first song, "Oh, What a Night." Quickly, scores of young seniors rock-and-rolled on the dance floor. Appropriately, the song brought the crowd back to yesteryear, at the same time glorifying and exalting our fiftieth anniversary in the wonderful way that only music can.

DANCING

The first couples on the floor danced so beautifully, one would've thought they married right after Midwood. (Only 2 percent of those who met in high school end up not divorcing.) The dance floor was so crammed that seniors practically fought for space. Admirably, about a half-dozen alumni in bad need of joint replacements teeter-tottered to the music. To my surprise, when the music slowed, many couples actually danced cheek to cheek, which back in high school for most guys I knew, was always a form of *floor play*. On the sidelines, my mind wandered to other types of dancing, the kinds that don't occur to music but to the rhythms of life, or a metaphor for life's passages.

In kindergarten we learned to play with others and assimilated the basic social movements to get along. As we navigated the steps through school, the dance patterns with friends, dating, and responsibilities became more complex. Quickly you wise up to the fact that you can't call many of the melodies you must dance to. I well remember my first job in a supermarket, where I rhythmically had to follow my boss's example of stamping prices and hustling aisle to aisle stocking merchandise.

Everyday interrelationships, choreographed over time, evolve into established routines. We dance in countless relationships. How we execute these steps determines our successes and failures. Ben Franklin said, "The most important dance in life for success is getting along with people." He never said it, but it gets more credence using his name rather than mine.

In marriage, sometimes we find the dance that once was so stimulating can become routine and boring. People generally dislike change, but they hate repetitiveness and boredom even more. "As lust fades and interests grow apart, it's the lack of friendship and selflessness that troubles marriages"—paraphrasing Nietzsche. To prevent significant others from looking for their excitement elsewhere, you have to find renewed interests. Life is about growth and change and is reflected by the steps we take along the journey. Despite what young people may think, being attractive to others doesn't entirely diminish with age.

Over time a couple's dance goes through adjustments, as relationships and love transform. In addition to some needing joint replacements or being slowed by age, many seniors have experienced drastic changes and hoof it very differently later in life.

That night, catching up with classmates, I found the majority were in long-term relationships. Some were divorced, while a few became widows or widowers. Also, as one might expect, a handful at the reunion sought romance. While observing classmates' interactions, I thought I could decipher through their conversations, body language, and hearing their unspoken words the types of relationships they were in.

For those who became single, anguish and bitterness often crept into their conversations. A few without companions bemoaned the loneliness of their situation. Loneliness is far from a rare and curious circumstance. It often can be a central, even inevitable happening. Nevertheless, for those in this age group, it is not uncommon for it to rear its ugly head. One might think it best if those companionless get together, but when "lonely people speak to each other, often they can make the other lonelier" (Hellman).

BUTLERS IN MY HOUSE

My digressions were suddenly jarred by a series of shoulder taps. Instantly, I turned and saw Paul Butler's signature smile explode. At once, I was transported back in time to the apartment building where we grew up. Our building, like thousands of others in Brooklyn, had six floors. Both of us also attended the University of Buffalo and became members of the same fraternity. Paul, however, pledged AEPI one year after me. I still remember how pissed he was after I assigned Paul this pledge task: "Since you really are a Butler, I want you to shovel my driveway every time it snows." Remember, it was Buffalo!

After Paul told about living in sunny Sausalito, California, and what was going on in his life, we segued back to our six-story building. Paul lived in 4J, and I lived in 6J; my family lived two stories directly above his. It seemed our building had more than its share of crazies. And with the sheer numbers of kids, we never had to go outside to play.

Looking out our windows was a favorite pastime. Our building faced directly opposite another six-story apartment building on East Twenty-Seventh Street. The side street, Campus Road, was part of Brooklyn College. On any given day, there were about a dozen voyeurs from each building looking out their windows, gawking at the people and activity below.

There was always commotion on the streets. For example, after school in late spring, there'd be Spalding stickball games, pronounced "spaldeen" by Brooklynites. These games would be regularly interrupted by the horns of irate drivers. Droves of co-eds walked to and from the college. Emerging teenage hormones greatly influenced how you'd check out these bouncing untouchables. On sidewalks below, hordes of mothers with their baby carriages took time out from chores to chitchat.

Residents leaning out windows bellowed strident exchanges and swapped small talk from one side of the street to the other. Each mother had a special ritual of calling her child home. My mother, the only person who called me by my complete first name, screamed "Ronald!" at the top of her lungs. You could hear her blocks away. My friends always loved to impersonate her. Mrs. Butler had the most amazing two-fingered, high-pitched, shrill whistle imaginable.

One afternoon I looked out my 6J window and noticed Paul Butler straight below me, sticking his head out. Being especially playful and a foot taller than Paul, I spit out my window, attempting to hit Paul's noodle just for kicks. Since there was a breeze and being new to the game, I missed on my first salivary attempt. Always trying to improve, I redirected my spit, allowing for the vagaries of the wind. Then, splat! Paul had no idea what hit him. He touched his head, perhaps thinking bird shit. Relieved it wasn't, Paul continued to watch the neighborhood from his perch. After a few minutes, I continued my target practice, though never hitting him again. After telling my friends of this new activity, I looked forward to increasing my expectorating skills. Mrs. Butler, like many parents, also liked looking out the window. However, there was an unspoken law: "Never, ever mess with a parent."

One day my mother forced me to stay home because I had a miserable cold and was coughing phlegm. This same day Paul's four-years-older brother, Jerry, stuck his head out. I could easily determine from the size of his dome it wasn't little Paul's. Totally bored, I thought, "Should I?" It seemed exciting—a reasonable shot, a bigger skull, and only a slight wind. Additionally, my friends would go bonkers hearing what I did. However, if caught, I knew big brother would literally beat the crap out of me. He was a Hood, which meant fisticuffs were his method of communication, especially with younger kids. I decided, what the heck, he'd never know—and what a rush. Since conditions were almost perfect, with mucous from my cold expediting, I filled my throat with a nice glob of phlegm and aimed. Figuring in the almost nonexistent wind, I spit the thick glob a drop to the right, never expecting it to nail the Hood. As I watched the phlegm descend, picking up speed from its sixth-story launch and heading directly at big brother's head, I couldn't believe what was happening! Bull's-eye—splat. Jerry Butler flinched, put his hand to his head, and immediately looked up. Though I dove inside, he knew! His younger brother must have tipped him off. Suddenly I felt a whole lot sicker!

I laid low for months, keeping away from the Butlers at all costs, and of course didn't go near my window. Eventually, when I did look out, they were never there. Starting to feel I got away with it, I began to relax, especially when I saw them in the street and elevators. Not a word was ever mentioned about my nasty spit bombs.

Many moons later on a perfect afternoon, I spotted little bro Butler slightly peeking his head out. I thought, "Maybe, just maybe—they really didn't know." Again, I couldn't resist the fun of Sal's salivary assaults. Sal is my nickname from Salmonson. However, this time it seemed little Paul was on to me, because he barely stuck his head out and unexpectedly kept bobbing his head around. After I was sure it wasn't Mrs. Butler or big brother, I rubbernecked like a giraffe out my window, leaning out as far as possible. While in this precariously outstretched position, I began my salivary offensive, but this time came up empty due to Paul's ducking and jerking. At the same moment and unbeknownst to me, the older Butler went on the roof with a pot of liquid ammunition. As I was fully extended, big brother dumped an entire pot of urine on my head! That retaliatory response effectively concluded my spitting activities, although I did become a dentist.

I've told this true story many times but never divulged what happened afterward. Here goes—I immediately went to the bathroom, towel in hand to wash my hair. Unfortunately, as luck would have it, I was greeted by my mother, also wanting to use the washroom. Since I completely reeked from urine, she said, "You smell... awful. Smells like...smells almost like urine! What's going on here?"

"I'm going to wash my hair, Ma," this eleven-year-old answered.

"How'd ya get that in your hair? Is it really urine? Get in the shower right this second. Who did this to you?" She hounded.

Obviously, I couldn't tell her that someone urinated on my head or someone dumped a bucket of urine on my head. She would've been pissed. Nevertheless, after she repeatedly threatened and badgered me, I had no choice but to confess. "I was just spitting out the window, and it accidentally landed on someone."

"What does spitting have to do with that disgusting odor coming from your hair?" she asked.

Astonishingly, after a few seconds, she got the picture, "It really is urine!" she shrieked.

Clearly this was, beyond doubt, my mother's first urinalysis.

"Who did it?" she asked.

"The Butlers did it," I replied.

After giving my mother this cliché from an old murder-movie mystery, she knew of course the culprits. However, despite being pissed off because I was pissed on, she cracked up laughing, trying hard not to. This made her laugh all the more. As her laughter subsided, a perplexing look slowly altered her face. Cognizant of this look from my many so-called past improper interactions with her (or so she thought), I realized she didn't have any idea what to do next. This unknowing look, which I knew so well, became par for the course in her lifelong dealings with me, who at times gave her great joys but often made her blood boil.

As I said good-bye to my childhood friend Paul, I thought about the countless number of people who've come and gone in my life. At my age, there's an unspoken thought that you don't know if you'll see these people again. Since I knew this most likely would be the last time with Butler, I told him how much he meant to me. People who are special should be told they're special. We stared fondly for a few seconds and then embraced. As we walked away, I brushed a tear from my eye. Paul was probably doing the same.

LUNATICS IN MY FLATBUSH NEIGHBORHOOD

Needing a break from this emotional parting, I went outside for some fresh air. Unfortunately, there was a small circle of smokers from the reunion puffing away. I realized some things haven't changed in fifty years. Inhaling deeply were two off-the-wall old pals, Marty Tochterman and Jimmy Platz, who lived on my block. I had always wondered what happened to them because they were such screwed-up misfits. In fact, they were so disturbed they didn't fit in with any of the other misfits. As kids, these two nut jobs should have worn T-shirts stating Proceed with Caution. That night, besides smoking, they were not too surprisingly passing a flask back and forth, which I assumed was alcohol and not the dietary supplement Ensure I hear senior citizens swig at times. Again, due to my scandalous past and never having graduated, they were flabbergasted seeing me.

Turmoil always lurked around Tochterman. As a kid he was a certified kleptomaniac with daring and eclectic tastes in thievery.

This big word, one of the first big words I was so proud to have learned, described Marty perfectly. It's a person who helps himself because he can't help himself.

The kids in my neighborhood gave nicknames to most people, whether they were pals, merchants, or parents. Since Marty Tochterman's name was way too long, I named him MT. I reasoned his initials were picture perfect because his pilfering often left a section in our candy store "MT."

I remember the time I was nine or ten being surprised when, after introducing Marty to my mother, she grinned and asked him, "How do you spell your last name?"

Later I picked her brain. "Ma, why did you ask MT—Marty, I mean—to spell his name?

My mother, knowing I was big into initials, smiled and then tried to suppress it. "I smiled because in Yiddish and German, Tochterman is a combination of 'tochter,' meaning 'daughter,' and of course, 'man' is 'man.'"

My mother, while trying to hold back her grin, saw mine explode and chuckled. Looking back, I'm sure my mother hoped I had some tact and wouldn't tell my friends about the derivation of MT's paradoxical last name. That of course lasted about an hour or two. As you can imagine, Marty went bonkers after discovering I was the reason why our friends more than smiled when they ad-*dressed* him as Daughterman. We didn't talk for months.

Before I go on, let me give you the backdrop as to why my parents were so perceptive to my fascination with initials. When I was about eight, I was the first in my family to realize the initials of my three-years-older sister, Arlene Sheila, spelled ASS. What's more, Arlene was born December 7, 1941, ten minutes before Japan bombed Pearl Harbor, which as you know signified the start of World War II for Americans.

After that discovery, whenever a quarrel erupted between us, I was emboldened by my bolstered *arse*-nal of verbal ammunition to *ass*-ault her. My concocted, on-target barrage might've sounded something like this:

"Besides starting World War II, which commemorated your infamous birth, Mom and Dad subconsciously labelled you an ASS for life. You were damaged goods from day one, born prematurely at seven months, squeezed out of the womb breech (I'm sure you know what that means) and appropriately given those initials." (Not bad for an eight-year-old.) After I'd let that sink in, and in case that wasn't enough, I might follow up with, "I can just picture the boys in junior high reacting to your monogramed sweaters."

That was the last time Arlene used or told anyone about her full name on her birth certificate. My parents, up to that time totally oblivious to their blunder, were beyond embarrassed. They could not console her for months or years. To this day I wonder how much this contributed to Arlene's many psychiatric visits.

Let's come back to talk about MT's cohort and best friend, Jimmy Platz. Platz, who gave the impression of growing every day, was six foot six and known, among other things, for his smoke rings, which seemed to waft out of the sky. They were breathtaking! He had the worst case of knock-knees imaginable. If his knees were straightened, he would have been seven feet tall, which would have matched up well with his size-seventeen shoes. As a kid, Jimmy wore thick, Coke bottle–like glasses with one eye covered, like a pirate's patch. The black patch attempted to correct his wandering eye, which I always wondered about. As a teenager Jimmy drank more beer than any kid in the neighborhood and also had a wandering eye when it came to the ladies. It was easy to determine what level of intoxication he reached simply by observing his method of locomotion. If he approached complete paralysis, he stood quietly and leaned against something for hours, like a lamppost or building. To boot, if Platz plotzed his size seventeens in your home, he maneuvered about like a rhinoceros in a ballet class.

Marty Tochterman and Jimmy Platz were taking drags of a small, thin cigarette they were passing back and forth and impishly asked, "Do you want a hit, some booze, or both?" and then laughed hysterically. Next they hammed it up by giving me animated high fives in slow motion. Tempted to toke at first, I declined, realizing if I did, I'd miss a good part of the reunion. After stumbling through the "good to see you" verbiage, Jimmy rasped, "We're probably the only ones still living in the old neighborhood. The Hasidic Jews and blacks are fightin' for our turf; not sure who'll win." As kids, their IQs, as they say, hovered around room temperature, and trouble constantly gravitated toward them.

During snowfalls, I'll never forget these two pals dangerously riding the back running boards of New York City's buses for kicks. They'd called it "yarring." They'd jump on, wave like crazy, and give you their biggest ear-to-ear grins. That night as I talked to them, I thought of the time-tested saying "The surprising thing about young fools is how many survive to become old fools" (Doug Larson). My sentiments exactly; people rarely change. What you see in someone when they're young is what you get later in life.

I believe in what many have said: "It is essential that a part of you not grow up." There's something special about childhood's spark and enthusiasm that you must take with you through life. It gives us our basic wonder and playfulness. "You're only given a little spark of madness—you mustn't lose it" (Robin Williams). Aristotle also agreed: "No great genius ever lived without some touch of madness." To this day, I gravitate toward people who are a little nuts or off in some way. I must find out why. I also believe in Montagu's line, "The idea is to die young as late as possible."

Obeying all rules is not always the way to go or you'll miss out on some fun. A certain amount of danger is essential to add excitement to life. Push the envelope. I certainly didn't do everything right—sometimes I went too far and paid the price—but there were lots of rushes. Take some risks, or, as Eleanor Roosevelt put it, "Do something every day that scares you."

THE GROUP I STAYED
AWAY FROM

At this fiftieth, as I'm sure at many others, there were a number of alumni who peaked in high school and were undoubtedly trying to relive their glory days. At ours, one clique of outcasts was loud and obnoxious while taking umpteen selfies of themselves. This ego-without-logic crowd, who was way too loud and thought too little, was using what I've amusingly heard dubbed "narcisticks" (a mixture of narcissism and selfie sticks). Watching them carry on made me think of Lucy Harper's tongue-in-cheek line, "The nicest thing about egotists—they don't talk about other people." Personally, I've never bought this line totally, because time and again I've heard egomaniacs put down other people.

On the other hand, I've always liked Mark Cuban's thought, "Don't force stupid people to be quiet. I want to know who the morons are." These sad souls don't have a clue their best days have long disappeared. I wonder if they still believe they're center stage, or are they deluding themselves? There are people whose watches stop at a certain hour and remain frozen there for life. Since it appears they view the world as they did back then, in all likelihood, in fifty years they haven't grown a lot.

It seemed a disproportionate number of women in this in-crowd, in their desperate attempt to turn back their odometers, had plastic surgeries and Botox. Unfortunately, for some of them, who were unable to recall they were grandmothers, their hoped-for cosmetic improvements, actually made their faces look preposterously frozen. This unnaturalness often was accentuated by their heavy use of shocking red lipstick, which, when applied to their surgically augmented, plump lips, frequently resulted in them being derisively dubbed "duck lips." Scary sight to see!

While watching this offensive inner circle whoop it up, a guy from this group who I knew from elementary school wandered by, attempting to strike up a conversation. I won't name this schlemiel because he was an absolute jerk, lacking every social skill. As far back as I could remember, he had an instinct for being unhappy, developed to an art form. Trying to be as tactful as I could, I nevertheless blew this loudmouthed, depressing energy sapper off and waved good-bye.

REFLECTIONS

I overheard some alumni talk about checking out the old neighborhood by revisiting the homes where they were raised. Gloria Gottlieb, a warm, brainy classmate whose face elegantly wore the years, showed her continuing perceptiveness, saying, "Going back and seeing my physical roots would give me so much comfort. I'll never forget old Brooklyn and the people who helped make me what I am today. I'm sure I'd feel like a traveler, returning after many years of wandering to the place I'd known as a child. It's humbling to remember the beginnings, where we all came from. I have this hunger to see my old stomping grounds and try to feel the good times we felt as kids. Nevertheless, we all know you cannot go home."

Listening to this woman made me realize that though I've traveled far from where I grew up, I'll never be able to shake or want to cut my Brooklyn ties. It'll always be a special place.

Renewing friendships was, of course, the main theme of this and every reunion. Unfailingly, all grads spent more time reconnecting with old friends and minimal time with others with whom they weren't palsy-walsy. From the night's conversations, you sensed classmates were now more candid and down to earth than as teens. Typically, most alumni didn't try to impress classmates with accomplishments. Many more self-deprecating lines were the norm, like Tochterman's wisecrack, "The closest I ever got to a 4.0 in school was my blood alcohol level." Reunions also give the opportunity to reflect on how you're doing and compare it to your high school years.

My off-the-cuff assessment of the participants was that this jam-packed room had a comparable number of doctors, lawyers, teachers, engineers, and assorted therapists. Most attendees went to college, had a modicum of success, and probably were better off than the no-shows. No one showed who I presumed was a real disaster—or they probably wouldn't have come. However, most of the Invisible People were still out of sight.

As I sauntered about, I came upon a heavyset woman I didn't know and heard her state, "I was told a few of the no-shows didn't attend because they wanted their high school memories to last forever. Evidently, they hold dear all those youthful, smiling faces etched in time." This insightful no-show comment caused me to pause and zero in on the night's attendees.

While no one goes untouched by time, I saw in many the resemblances of their former selves. An individual's personality and character don't disappear with age. It remains forever who you are. It's there, hidden behind the wrinkles and constantly withering physique.

On the other hand, when I now look in the mirror, I wonder, "Who's that?" I can't believe it's me. I wince seeing myself. I'm looking more like my grandfather than my father. I'll forever dread the ravages of time. Wouldn't it be great, at this stage in life, to go through our remaining days without mirrors and never letting anybody take our pictures? My mind and body don't match up, not even close. It slays me; this is what I look like, yet on the inside I feel *so differently*. How did it happen so fast? Where did the years go? Now, starting my eighth decade, I certainly realize a lifetime isn't a very long time!

Now don't get me wrong, I'm not a shallow individual who dwells on physicality. I certainly recognize aging is part of life, and no one can wear young men's clothes forever. Be that as it may, for most, one's mortality rears its ugly head more commonly with age. This is scary, but it also opens new perspectives for these "no spring chickens." With the passage of time, one frequently rethinks his or her priorities, often resulting in a "right now" sense of urgency.

The physical changes accompanying old age, on which modern-day society often heaps scorn, can be looked upon as preconditions for life's winter years, necessary characteristics needed to be socially productive. What is open to interpretation is the possible positive purposes for these changes. What if they're understood as a form of preparation (not unlike adolescence) for a new life as an elder of the community?

There are places worldwide where getting old is something to look forward to. The United States possibly could be in the minority of countries that doesn't look up to seniors. Typically, in many societies, the elderly are regarded with respect because of their knowledge. By virtue of their vast experience, they've dealt with a multiplicity of problems. Old age comes with an increased tolerance to people and circumstances. Therefore, the elderly can more readily advise and pave the way for others. Consequently, due to their extended insights, they can in theory more easily solve problems. That's why older people often are sent to peace negotiations. There's an African saying about the passing of a revered senior: "The death of an old person is like the loss of a library."

While I'm not exactly calling this time of life Eldertopia, there are numerous benefits to aging. James Taylor's perspective in song, "Since we're on our way down, might as well enjoy the ride," gives a different way of looking at things. Fortuitously, as I walked around the ballroom, I overheard a woman respond to the question, "What was the best time of your life?"

"Right now!" she answered emphatically. Expounding upon her response, she said, "This is a time of leisure and freedom to explore whatever I wish. I'm watching my children realize their dreams, and my grandchildren are starting to blossom. Nowadays, I'm surrounded by cherished friends who have withstood the test of time. At this moment I'm enjoying independence, enabling me to be self-indulgent whenever I want. Right now, I'm very appreciative of life."

Another woman chimed in, "I totally agree. I'm free from all those deadlines, time limits, and unnatural urgencies of my early days."

One fellow, battling a recurrence of cancer said, "You have no promises you'll see all the seasons of your life or even one more day. So live for today, and say all the things you want your loved ones to remember."

Old age comes with reduced responsibilities and fewer expectations. This contributes to having more inner peace. Senior citizens' battles have been waged and decisions made. They don't have to push, strive, and surmount the dizzying bustle that can suffocate younger people. They don't have huge expectations for their futures, as they've done basically all they could already. They also can keep their expenditures down, as they don't have to spend on trendy clothes, shoes, or electronics, to name just a few examples.

On the other hand, who hasn't looked at someone on TV, in newspapers, in a magazine, and so on and thought, "Do I look as old as that guy?" Why is this built into our defense system—that we usually think we're younger looking than the person we're comparing ourselves to?

The other day, I thought about something I've rarely heard discussed—the quality of a person's aging organs beneath his skin. While performing oral surgery on a ninety-year-old the other day,

I couldn't help but notice the patient's thin, friable tissues. If this is happening in his oral cavity, logic would tell me, it's occurring throughout his body. In this regard, since I look so old externally, is it ridiculous for me to hope my internal organs are faring better than my external anatomy?

Recently, D. Belsky, a Duke University physician, compared eighteen medical factors (blood pressure, lung function, DNA integrity, etc.) trying to calculate the physiological internal ages of his subjects. Surprisingly to me, he found people were biologically at different ages, despite being the same age chronologically. Comparing the slower- and faster-aging groups, he discovered, amazingly, 80 percent of the aging factors weren't genetic and were therefore well within an individual's control: weight, healthy diet, exercise, and stress reduction. Therefore, by applying his findings, which must start at an early age, one should be able to improve the age of his or her internal organs, thus ensuring a better and longer quality of life.

SENIOR CITIZEN TRENDS

Most alumni spoke of life being much simpler back then. That's how nostalgia works. "Nostalgia," coined in the 1680s, described a medical pathology of a painful longing for home. In every generation it seems the world perceives it was better forty years ago than the present. Idealizing the past is deeply ingrained in our species. The phrase "the good old days" appeared in print in 1726, shortly after print itself appeared.

As I passed a table of women, I heard a down-and-out lady quote John Lennon: "Life's what happens while you're busy making other plans." Resuming, she said, "I never expected to hear of the 'sandwich generation,' let alone be the foremost player in it, until recently. I'm simultaneously being squeezed between my grown kids living at home because they can't find work and an elderly mother who's in cognitive no-man's land, also living with us. Caring for the elderly is like parenting toddlers, only they get worse with time. I've definitely bit off more than I can chew."

Her classmate nearby stated, "The same thing is happening to me. I'm struggling to parent my aging parents and parent my own children. In addition, I'm trying to make a living and save for retirement, if I'll ever have one. And it's mostly women, 75 percent of the time, who are saddled with the responsibility. I don't have the money or hours in a day to deal with all this."

Listening closely to the conversation and wanting to give her two cents' worth was Wendy Wayne. In due course she said, "I have a different situation. I'd love to have meaningful interactions with my grandchildren but won't because I had my first daughter at thirty-eight. If my daughter waits, as many of her generation have, and has kids when I did, I'd be a grandmother at seventy-six. At that age, could I be the Nana I had hoped, having close relationships with my grandkids and being able to watch them so my daughter could devote more time to her career? Or will my daughter need to be taking care of me in addition to her own kids?"

"Grandparent deficit," applicably coined (Schrobsdorff), describes how having children late in life impacts on the special bonds among all three generations.

NINE O'CLOCK MEANDER

Needing a break, I strolled about and came across Alan Homel, a doubly special alumnus because he graduated Midwood and the University of Buffalo with me. Cutting past phony formalities, he unhappily revealed, "I retired from teaching twelve years ago but really was forced out. The system makes a teacher who's usually at the top of his game an offer he can't refuse, especially at fifty-five with thirty years on the job. If you do the retirement pension math, it doesn't pay to continue. Now I'm struggling. I've got little to do and feel I'm wasting away. Now at our age, with so many people fighting for jobs, you can't get a decent one. I should have tried harder in Buffalo, where I started out predental, and been a dentist like you. You've got to go after the things you want while you're in your prime. Back then, I remember it was one of the hardest decisions I ever made—whether to stay the course and try harder or call it quits and move on. Then again, you never know till you get there whether it was worth the uphill climb."

Before I could say a word, Alan continued, "On top of being down, I can't sleep or concentrate. I have no energy, always tired. And the latest thing, if I stand up too quickly, I get dizzy."

Shaking my head and trying to lighten him up, I responded, "How strange. The other day my son said when he smokes two joints, he feels exactly the same way."

Distressingly, I was particularly thrown off guard when Homel didn't smile whatsoever, as he would have in the good old days. He appeared to be listening but really wasn't. He kept his eyes focused on me, but something in his expression indicated his mind was elsewhere. He rambled, "Ron, as you can see, I don't exactly have my shit together these days. Would you be straight with me? Have you ever thought of suicide?"

Trying hard to reduce Alan's despair, my mind went out to lunch. Floundering to say something that might alleviate his depression, I resorted to humor as I usually do and babbled, "No, do you think I should?"

Seriously, I referred Alan to a good friend, a psychiatrist who specialized in depression. The only drawback is that I think the shrink is depressed himself and may have an alcohol problem. The therapist once told me his favorite motto: "A drink a day keeps the shrink away."

PROBLEMS OF THE AGE

A few downtrodden classmates spoke of the many difficulties they faced as they approached their eighth decade. Anyone in this age group can attest to the struggles with aching joints, fading eyesight, hearing, and the like. Hall of fame basketball player Charles Barkley, speaking on the passage of time, wisecracked, "Father Time has never been defeated." An alumnus said, "I'm losing my resilience to cope with problems. As each day passes, the world becomes more incomprehensible and complex, like technology, for example." Others talked about their health being broken or their not-getting-any-younger bodies failing to cooperate as before.

Among many, sadness was apparent as classmates spoke of spouses or even children dying. How unspeakable it is to get invested in living things that you outlive. Rabbi Marc Gellman said, "Grief is the price we pay for love. The deeper the love, the deeper the grief. You surely wouldn't agree to the deal in which you loved less in order to grieve less. Grief is the cost of love we willingly accept when we open our lives to loving others." One widow lamented, "No one ever told me grief felt so much like fear. Grief, like many things, can't be shared; everyone carries it his or her own way." These unattached schoolmates have long and emptier days.

From the beginning of our life, the number of social contacts increases with time. Our universe overlaps with the orbits of many others, additionally broadening our connections. On the other hand, in general, as our journey winds down, the opposite happens. People can become isolated, socially and emotionally. This may come about because individuals in their seventh decade typically retire from the work force, resulting in the loss of many business associates they've spent considerable time with. At this time, it's common for these seniors' children to marry or relocate. Others lose social contacts as friends and extended family move to retirement communities, while others pass on. The subject of loneliness came up at this reunion more than I expected, especially among the companionless.

Terrible, unimaginable things happen in the course of one's life. We can never predict when and where. Though we try to make our foundations stable, we know we're vulnerable. All of us are fearful of any loss, but everyone realizes sorrow and wreckage are part of the passage. No one emerges unscathed. We learn the lessons of human resilience; we will always be knocked down. It's getting up and going on that count.

From my experience, the only people who usually don't have any existential worries are those who are less than ten years old. The rest of us know too much. Thinking back, maybe one of the definitions of youth is "a life untouched by tragedy" (Alfred Whitehead).

A distant relative of mine, Karen Salmansohn (a number of my cousins spell their surname differently), came up with this spot-on quotation most of us would agree with: "It's kinda funny how being old doesn't seem so old now that I am old." When you were young,

I'm sure you knew many people who viewed retirees in the same manner as aging horses being put out to pasture. At this festive event, some classmates complained about becoming invisible in a world obsessed with youth. "Growing old is like being increasingly penalized for a crime you haven't committed" (A. Powell). Or as William James said, "Aging is a slow, reluctant march into enemy territory."

Of late I feel the hands of time ticking more rapidly, and I'm running out of time, or, as my college roommate, Barry Cohen, put it so eloquently, "It's like being on a moving walkway at an airport. We can't even slow down our walk. It won't matter." At this point in time, I'm finding that death's door, once so distant, doesn't seem so distant. Yogi Berra, who turned ninety before he died, said, "The future ain't what it used to be. It got late early out there."

Apropos of those suffering from the loss of a loved one, we instinctively feel empathy and compassion for those in mourning. A number of these unfortunate souls, who've lost someone they've deeply cared about, frequently find themselves depressed. Additionally, they experience the loss of not being lovingly cared for. One woman lamented, "Life has put me where I don't want to be. My house now echoes the voice of a man who isn't there." Some who've lost loved ones tumble into an abyss of extreme sorrow, but most, fortunately, demonstrate the resilience of the human spirit.

On a positive note, for those there that night who were despondent, a Southampton University study confirmed, "A good wallow of the past can alleviate depression and make the reminiscing party feel less alone."

A TOUCH OF MADOFF

I was startled out of my thoughts by a down-in-the-dumps, very familiar bald guy. As I stared, our eyes met. It was Steve O'Brien! Steve's downtrodden demeanor, I surmised, resulted from his recent criminal indictments, which headlined every New York newspaper: "O'Brien Scam Artist Charged in Billion-Dollar Madoff-Like Scheme."

While Steve's downtrodden mannerisms conveyed the mood that he was aware this would be the last time he'd see his fellow classmates, I could think only of the good times we shared. I'm sure he wasn't reflecting on those raucous occasions we partied to. Steve was now awaiting sentencing and could spend the rest of his life in prison. He and his partner were charged with stealing more than one billion dollars from charities, pension plans, and universities. As teens we were very close but with time drifted apart. This evening he certainly didn't act like the O'Brien of old, when he was the life of the party and radiated an aura of celebrity. That night many, it seemed, were giving Steve furtive looks, not so slyly, from afar.

Growing up with no meat on our bones and no money, Steve and I played numerous sports together. He was a great competitor with a wonderful sense of humor. More importantly, he was a good friend. After high school, we were roommates at the University of Buffalo for three years. Yet looking back, there were signs.

Steve studied very little and got by through cheating and using people. During a Chemistry 101 final, Steve could've received an Oscar for his outrageous, deceitful performance. In a cavernous lecture hall, hundreds of students were taking their exams, proctored by teaching assistants (TAs). Midway through the test, a short TA, who was watching O'Brien cheat, tapped him on the shoulder and quietly asked him to leave. After slowly rising, Steve then bent down to get into the TA's face and, at the top of his lungs, bellowed so loudly that every student stopped the test to witness the exchange. "You have the audacity in front of my classmates and friends to accuse me of cheating!" Steve screamed. The TA, taken totally off guard, was shocked by Steve's rebuttal and even appeared to cringe. Surprisingly, however, the TA allowed him to finish the final. The story went viral, even before there was such a concept.

Steve's greatest attribute, a quality rarely discussed and the one that brought about his downfall, was picking partners. In addition to exploiting friends and fraternity brothers, he chose his wife perhaps because she happened to come from money. After college, his father-in-law positioned Steve in puts and calls, a new financial venture that jump-started his fortune. Later, Steve latched on to a brilliant, not-so-kosher business associate who further catapulted his riches. Their partnership eventually led to a five-floor Wall Street investment firm, which enabled them to buy a controlling interest in a New York professional hockey team, with Steve becoming president. However, ironically, after the firm was indicted for embezzlement, his partner turned state's evidence against Steve in the attempt to reduce his own sentence.

We spoke at length of high school, friends, romance, and our Buffalo years. Our blissful, side-splitting college memories took place in a fairy-tale setting most people could only dream about. These treasured happenings transpired in a venue with very few restraints. Now they felt bittersweet, because Steve knew he would probably be spending the rest of his life in jail. His last words to me before incarceration were, "Ron, I learned money never brings happiness."

After hugging, I left thinking my one small investment with Steve wasn't pocketed and even made a few bucks, adding to our friendship. Many victims worked very hard for their money and played by the rules. I certainly recognize justice must be served for this reprehensible thievery, still affecting untold numbers. "When you choose the behavior, you choose the consequences" (Dr. Phil McGraw). And yes, I do hope to visit him in jail.

SOMBER MOMENTS

Sparkling lights emanating from a nearby table piqued my interest. Someone's birthday was being celebrated with scores of glittering candles. The reunion seemed like an unusual place for this festivity, but after thinking about it, why not? In fact, it added to the gaiety of the night. Loosened by a few drinks and dazzled by the lights, I recalled the line, "You know you're old when the candles cost more than the cake."

The birthday celebrant, sitting with his significant other, looked familiar, though he looked out of it. His clothes, although somewhat disheveled, didn't bother me as much as his eyes. Though once vibrant I'm sure, his eyes appeared vacuous; I've seen this in those cognitively impaired. As I stared, my mind traveled back in time, and then it hit me—Larry Schwartz. I remembered playing punch ball as kids and taking a class in journalism together. I heard through the grapevine Larry earned his PhD in English and became a well-known sportswriter.

Therefore, I was not surprised he didn't recognize me or that his companion did the talking. Being sensitized to dementia, as the specter runs in my family, I speculated Larry was in the early stages of Alzheimer's. In the past, I've speculated how patients with dementia deal with the confusion of living in a world that does not make much sense; their bygone days being so cloudy or forgotten and the future so foreboding. Now as I travel down memory lane and compare Larry's mental deterioration with what he was, the awareness hits: a brain once filled with such unlimited potential, now gone forever. Studying this formerly respected sportswriter, I thought about his inevitable, inescapable cognitive deterioration. "So long, old pal." This begged the age-old question, is it better to age poorly than not age at all?

My thoughts regarding Larry were sidetracked by another familiar alumnus who also was watching the brightly illuminated birthday scene. I couldn't help but notice the gentleman's helmet of white hair, lightened by the flaming candles. After transforming his full-bodied titanium headdress to the pitch-black color of yesteryear and ironing out a few facial wrinkles, I recalled the guy. It was Alan Silver, whose nickname at Midwood was Blackie. It was hairy seeing him after all these years, especially after he grinned and said, "Now everyone calls me Whitey." After the typical how-you-been verbiage, we talked of Larry, the birthday cake, and dementia.

Silver (alias Whitey, Blackie) said, "Funny, seeing Larry's cake reminded me of my own birthday, which was yesterday. My family however, used only seven candles, so I guess I taught them how to save some money." While looking at Larry, he whispered to me, making sure Schwartz didn't hear, "At our age, I guess we all wonder if we're showing signs of Alzheimer's."

"Ironically, today is my half birthday," I said. After Alan squinted and gave me that characteristic "what are you talking about" look, I continued with, "I think once you're collecting social security, you should celebrate birthdays semiannually. Given that we're running out of them, it would be neat to have them twice a year.

Also, in view of the fact that most of us party less, it would be cool to have another excuse to party more. This could lead to a spin-off in birthday merchandising. You'd be able to sell birthday cards and cakes twice a year."

My whimsical thoughts were interrupted by our class president thumping the microphone. "Attention, please; attention, please." After several perfunctory remarks and worthy acknowledgments, he said, "I'd like to say just a couple of things and let you go back to having fun." His first thought-provoking quote was absolutely on the money: "Isn't it ironic that we spend our school days yearning to graduate and our remaining days waxing nostalgic about our school days?" (Isobel Waxman).

After pausing to let that thought sink in, he somberly said, "At this juncture I'd like a moment of silence for those classmates who are no longer with us." Instantly, I thought of Way-Out Willie Diamond, who died when he was fourteen. Willie was a nut job, a fun, schoolyard pal, with whom I played ball almost every day. He got his label from always pushing the envelope, thinking he was immune to death. He, like all kids, lived life as though our sunny days wouldn't end. Kids aren't supposed to die! It goes against all the rules of nature. It wasn't fair, it was scary, and it shook up every kid in our neighborhood. (An autopsy revealed an enlarged heart caused his death.) We experienced death for the first time when it put its hand upon someone we loved.

The death of Wild Willie impacted me in ways my parents, teachers, and other adults could not have understood. Friends at that age seemed as important as family. When Willie died, my entire world and belief system were shaken to its core. No longer thinking the end of life happens only to old people, I experienced death's realities and my own mortality. No one wants to die, except maybe people who are suffering, such as the terminally ill or those contemplating suicide. Even people who want to go to heaven don't want to die to get there. Yet death is the destination we all share.

For quite a while, I was consumed by his passing. I finally came out of this funk after realizing if I spent all this time worrying about dying, life wasn't going to be much fun.

Thinking back to my self-absorbed state in high school, I don't recall thinking much about Wild Willie's parents during their unimaginable ordeal. Now I do. There's nothing as unnatural as a parent burying a child. Even thinking about it triggers some sort of defense mechanism that attempts to stop you from envisioning it. All cultures have words to describe the loss of family members. If a woman loses her husband, she's a widow; if the husband loses his spouse, he's a widower. In every civilization in the world, there are no words to describe the loss of a child; it is too painful to be put into words!

My father didn't give a whole lot of advice, but when he did, I listened. "In the circle of life, life is a gift we must give back," he said. "Willie would've wanted you to learn from his passing, not to waste your days, because you never know when your number is up. I liked him a lot. Out of all your friends, he seemed to have it most together." It's not easy to be taught a lesson in life when adversity strikes, but my dad gave me these words of wisdom I'll always revere.

Willie was a terrific kid, and I was close to him, but not that close. Looking back, I'm certain I felt closer to him in death than I ever did in life. He definitely wasn't faultless. I never told my father the many things Willie and I did we weren't proud of. What's more, this was the first time I heard a very significant person, my dad, essentially say that after people die, you remember them as being better than they were when they were alive.

Through my life, whether it would be at eulogies or in passing conversations, a newly deceased is often lauded with over-the-top praises and exaggerations. You'd think he was being immortalized for sainthood. Accordingly, can you imagine how good I'm going to be after I'm laid to rest?

Though I know people are trying to soften the blow for relatives of the deceased, I'm often amazed how far some of these overly enthusiastic praises push the envelope. Reflecting, I think there's a honeymoon period after someone dies when nothing bad is said about the deceased. The length of the period during which we sing praises is directly proportional to how virtuous and honorable they were. Conversely, if the person was a total loser, the honeymoon time is inversely proportional before some bad-mouthing might surface.

At this point in time, I certainly recognize I'm running out of time and realize there are no promises, as the saying goes, how long I'll be looking down at the right side of the grass. For this reason, I'm trying to live for today and say all the things I want my loved ones to remember. I am truly mindful to push myself to appreciate every day. "Don't regret growing older; it's a privilege denied to many" (anonymous).

Before I pass from death, the topic unearthed an eerie memory of my first graveyard visit. When I was about five, I remember walking down a very narrow one-way cemetery lane, holding my father's hand. Being precocious, I picked up on the mourners' demeanors, expressing their somber, deep-seated uneasiness. I also remember being afraid to witness my first dead body and paradoxically disappointed when my father said, "You won't be seeing Uncle Sid because he's already in a sealed coffin." I also recall this five-year-old thinking that the cemetery was really a noiseless, spacious neighborhood for those who've departed.

My parents schlepped me along for the burial of Uncle Sid, whom I thought of as predead with one foot in the grave while he was alive. This was before I had any idea what a dead person looked like. Prior to undertaking the trip for the undertaking, I asked my mom, "How should I act, and what do you do there?"

She forewarned, "It's a sad time and place. Be on your best behavior. Watch your older cousin, Peter, and act like him."

My mother was a wailer, possibly could've led the league in howling. Because of this, I wasn't surprised when she uncontrollably bawled and screamed at the gravesite. Her raucous, wake-the-dead antics upset and embarrassed me big time. Therefore, as she put on her show, I sneaked a half block away and hid behind a tombstone.

My father, who had been watching, caught up with me and ordered me back. While walking hand in hand, I surprisingly was taken aback when he started laughing. "What's so funny?" I asked. He pointed up to a one-way street sign. A prankster had bent the sign so it pointed directly into the ground. I remember grinning ear to ear because I was so proud I got my first adult joke, and to this day I remember my father's beaming face. These eternally imprinted memories, occurring eons ago, come to life, reliving my first encounters with death.

LOVE REAWAKENING

In a secluded corner, oblivious to the world, were two former high school flames, Howie Harris and Carol Amato. The backdrop was surreal: in a dreamlike setting, two almost seventy-year-olds staring into each other's eyes, hands and knees pretty much touching. It had been more than fifty years since they last dated. In your mind's eye, picture a balding, potbellied senior going gaga over an *alta cocker* (literally translates "old shit") teary-eyed grandmother. The scene was comically lovey-dovey. Now envision puffy Howie bursting out of his faded, three-sizes-too-small Midwood varsity track jacket and Carol's mascara running out of control down her cheeks. She looked like a girl who'd just played with her mother's makeup. The scene—priceless.

About a month earlier, Howie, a reunion committee member, revealed to me he was eagerly looking forward to this milestone. Howie, divorced seven years, had excitedly discovered his first love, Carol, would be attending. He also learned she had lost her husband to cancer a year ago.

They dated passionately in their senior year, loving each other with the fierce, timeless conviction of teenagers. Despite fumbling with each other's buttons, they ended up more than hurting one another. Eventually they split due to religious, educational, and financial differences. Carol came from a poor family, was forced to work full time, and couldn't afford college. Howie's father had cautioned, "Love endures only when lovers love many things together, not merely each other."

Howie confided to me, "I'm really a basket case about seeing Carol. Of late, not a day goes by that I'm not haunted by a vague, powerful sense of regret of what I allowed myself to lose. She was my first love, and I never really got over her. I wonder what she looks like, if the years have been kind, and what she'll think of me. What do I say to her? Look at me; I'm a nervous wreck. I'm crippled by the fear she won't give me the time of day. How could she? I look like my father, an old, fat, bald guy. I'm so crazed, I even talked to my psychiatrist about her.

"Gratefully, the shrink eased my mind, saying, 'In life, you fall in love with perhaps a handful of people, and a handful fall in love with you. But the affections are rarely mutual or at the same time. When it happens, it's almost foolish to let such a coincidence pass and not act on it. It's impossible to love someone like Carol and totally part. Although you wish you could let it go, it persists subconsciously. It's truly love when the pain doesn't fade and the scars don't heal.'"

Trying to ease his concerns, I said, "Howie, it's only natural to worry about those extra pounds or your receding hairline. Keep in mind, when reconnecting with old friends, looks aren't everything. After a few minutes, you'll see the person as he or she was. Everyone will be looking through rose-colored glasses."

Howie lamented, "Thinking back, as a kid my objective was perfection. I now know love changes with time. I'm scared stiff about sex. That's funny; I guess subconsciously I used that word—stiff—because I'm worried about that too. Haven't had it in quite a while. Maybe I should take a refresher course. Even now, after all these years, she reappears in my thoughts, and it still hurts. How I wish she knew…I'm sure anticipating the reunion intensified my feelings, but that aching in the center of my chest when I think about her never really went away. We're hitting seventy, in the autumn of our years. I've never passed this way before, don't have a clue how to act."

"Be natural," I suggested. "Wear your heart on your sleeve, and be vulnerable. It's risky, but anything of value emerges from going deep and tapping your innermost thoughts. If the temperature is rising, run the gamble of exposing your feelings. Don't worry about sex. Everyone knows the tools of love wear down. If you're not willing to take the chance, then you don't want it badly enough. Have the guts to stake everything on it."

Unquestionably, I made it my business to seek them out, especially to get a glimpse of Carol, hoping the two were on the make. After locating them, you couldn't help but notice the genuine warmth of Carol's smile and the twinkling in both their eyes. It was obvious. They still had a thing for each other. As I swung by intermittently, watching these former lovebirds, my gut feeling was, it may work!

Later that night, Kramer took photographs of our close-knit friends. While waiting for the group to assemble, I asked Howie, "How's it going with Carol?"

He exclaimed, "I was so nervous, I had to wait an hour for my stomach to stop its nervous acrobatics. After rounding up all my courage and making sure she was alone, I faintheartedly approached her but couldn't do anything but stare. Tongue tied and not knowing what to say, I timidly and absurdly asked, 'How've you been?'"

Carol answered, "Fine, I guess," while simultaneously shaking her head and raising her eyebrows at the abject, meaningless question. As if fifty years could be compressed into a short answer.

"I guess what I mean is, how are you really?" Howie again asked, this time feeling a little small after he became conscious of what a boneheaded question it was, trying to recover.

"I'm decent. Like everyone else, hit some rough patches here and there. A year ago, burying my husband was more than tough, but these days I'm trying hard to make all those tears disappear," she answered candidly, like an even-tempered trouper.

"Ron," Howie continued, "boy, was I surprised to see that she's still so down to earth, just like in high school. As soon as I recognized she's the same old Carol, I started to relax and sensed the years melting away."

After the photos, which took much longer than expected because everyone wanted a keepsake, Howie said to me, "Listen, I want to get back to Carol; I'm sure you understand. We'll get together for lunch next week, and I'll tell you how the rest of the night went."

GERIATRIC FLIRTATIONS

Few events in life are as rife with potential romantic opportunities as reunions, where old flames can be relit. A handful of alumni even entertained the thoughts of "What if? If only..." when thinking of former classmates. Some attendees whose marriages might've been fraying appeared on the prowl and perhaps followed through. Adding to the intrigue, a few former ugly ducklings came to the event as swans.

As I wandered about, one stunning woman, Carla Minkoff (who Kramer said was single after three marriages), had a few guys fawning after her. This caused me to wonder what kinds of attributes these people possess to make them desirable to multiple mates. Preposterously, as I watched her sashay about with two followers in tow, she stopped in front of a handsome guy and, using her never-ending charm, gushed coquettishly, "I was so infatuated with you in high school."

The still-good-looking alumnus, with a bottle of beer in hand, seemed out of it. Maybe liquored up, stoned, or both, he slurred, "Honey, I'm single now. Just got divorced from my second wife and still looking for the right one. Love to buy you a drink and catch up."

Thereupon, Carla flaunted her knockout smile and said, "Maybe at the next reunion." She then laughed infectiously as she blew him a kiss and moved on, leaving no doubts about it.

Later, I heard a classy classmate flirt with a onetime nerd who had now blossomed, give her philosophy on love affairs, and divulge to him, "The truth is, every potential love or long-term mate is gonna hurt you. You just got to find the one worth the suffering."

Nearby, some guy who had been listening responded, "Wow, never heard anyone break it down like that; loved it. Just lost my wife about a year ago after forty years of marriage. Recently started dating again but hate all the crap that goes with it. I'm no Einstein, have some smarts, got some flaws, got some baggage, but who doesn't? Love to hear more of your thoughts. Could we get some coffee afterward?"

Late in life, everyone knows a potential love carries a ton of baggage, and no one is perfect in any sense. So the question arises, if they both aren't perfect, how could they now be perfect for each other?

A PISSER AT THE URINAL

I didn't want to miss a moment of the reunion, but nature called. After waiting too long, I dashed to the restroom and just made it. As I was unzipping my fly, I was stopped by my lifelong friend Fred March. He had just zipped up and extended his hand to shake, after shaking something else. "I ain't touching that," I said, lunging for the closest urinal. On the other hand, as he withdrew his hand, he couldn't control his signature smile. He had the kind that suffused every part of his face—his eyes, cheeks, lips. There was even a dimple. His knockout smile just exploded.

Fred and I competed for a starting position in the backcourt for Midwood's basketball team. He was the consummate teammate and a pleasure to be around. Three hours a day, we'd guard—make that "kill"—each other on the hardwood. If I beat him on a play, he'd give the warmest, most genuine smile imaginable. Next play, we'd go at each other again. To this day, we're close, now renewing our rivalry on the tennis courts. Fred is a freak of nature, six feet tall (hasn't shrunk), 145 pounds, still works out two hours a day, and runs marathons. Whether it's genetics or in combo with his heavy-duty workouts, Fred's body refuses to act its age.

One day, after Fred and I played doubles, he noticed I'd gained a few pounds and commented, "I know you went through hell with your hip and knee replacements and all that physical therapy, but you're getting to look a little puffy."

Without losing a beat, I repeated Red Skelton's line: "I get plenty of exercise lately by carrying the coffins of my friends who exercise."

Fred and I go way back to second grade. Show and Tell was our favorite homework assignment. Fred proudly beamed the day he brought his father's full-face picture that appeared on the front page of the *Daily News*. Little could he comprehend that his father, alias Johnny Bananas of Mafia infamy, was arrested for gambling and loan sharking. His father was also involved with Jack Molinas, a Columbia University basketball star who was incarcerated for five years (1964) for his role in the college basketball point-shaving scandals. After prison, Molinas was killed, a bullet to his head at age forty-three. Fred confided, "Growing up, I had the highest highs and the lowest lows; my father was always in and out of jail."

Maybe even more mind-bogglingly, he divulged, "My parents were married and divorced three times to each other!" His dad was also credited (?) with being one of New York's first pornographic movie suppliers. Fred revealed (I thought about using "exposed"), "Coming home from school, I'd be hungry but sometimes couldn't get near the refrigerator. The fridge was used as a movie screen for my dad's porn distributors."

Before the reunion, March and I agreed we wouldn't spend any significant time together because we still see each other socially. We agreed to use the event to reconnect with former friends.

HONORING A TEACHER

Reentering the vast ballroom, I was taken off guard because there was no music, and everyone again was listening to our class president. "We're in for a surprise tonight. I persuaded one of our favorite teachers, Mrs. Kaufman, to join us in traveling down memory lane. Lonnie, her son, who graduated with us and who many of you know, was crucial in convincing and transporting our honored guest." The class rose and applauded, as ninety-five-year-old, wispy-haired Mrs. Kaufman, aided by her cane and son, slowly made her way to center stage. The applause went on endlessly, gradually diminishing only after a wobbly and bashful Mrs. K waved her hand repeatedly, imploring the audience to stop.

The audience strained to hear Mrs. Kaufman's weak voice as she said, "I want to thank everyone for inviting me. It's both a pleasure and a privilege." She continued, "Most of you know Woody Allen graduated from Midwood a few years before your class. However, very few of you know Woody penned two of his famous quotes as a student here. The first I'd like to cite is one I might've followed subconsciously, as I get closer to being a centenarian: 'You can live to be a hundred if you give up all the things that make you want to live to be a hundred.'" She paused to let the chuckling subside, adding, "The second is particularly apropos to those present tonight: 'I had a terrible education. I attended a school for emotionally disturbed teachers.'"

Looking around, I couldn't help but notice every classmate's gleaming eyes. Resuming, she said, "Class, because these same teachers probably sculpted your lives, I'm sure this explains so many of your imperfections and inadequacies." The laughter from Mrs. Kaufman's clever quips triggered another standing ovation. Finishing, she waved good-bye, and, while slowly exiting, she stopped, faced the audience, and said, "See you in fifteen years, when I'll be back as a supercentennial. That'll make me 110, if you do the math." Then, while holding on to the cane's handle, she proceeded to kick the bottom of the cane up in the air, twirl it, and let it land, not unlike the old days of vaudeville. The roars that emanated from the unexpected playfulness of our former teacher still resonate!

Mrs. Kaufman, an exceptional, passionate math mentor, did much to improve the lives of her students. This quintessential educator made former students recall the handful of other teachers we placed on pedestals. "I like a teacher who gives you something to take home to think about besides homework" (Lily Tomlin). Dedicated, cream-of-the-crop teachers are always prized.

After Mrs. Kaufman's remarks, I spoke to her son, Lonnie, a fellow dentist whom I occasionally see at professional meetings. Though his mother was phenomenal, I always wondered how difficult it was for mother and son to be in the same school simultaneously, let alone high school. After chitchatting, Lonnie reflectively asked, "My mother and I could never fathom why you broke into Midwood."

Casting my eyes down, I said, "We were out of our minds. It was the rush, excitement, whatever. It started as a caper and escalated.

On the other hand, we felt we received the appropriate punishment for our stupidity. We paid the price and moved on. Nevertheless, it affected me greatly. It was an absolute disaster: searing shame, humiliation, and loss of dignity. Although, trying to be objective, what teenager hasn't made mistakes?" I then rambled on not too coherently about something or other, which we all tend to do when someone asks tough questions.

"After Midwood, where'd you finish high school?" Lonnie asked.

"New Utrecht. It was over an hour's trek. I had to take a train and bus to get there. Didn't know anyone; felt like a pariah because of my infamous reputation. But looking back, I was treated pretty decently."

Changing the still-awkward subject, I said to Lonnie, "I like asking people what high school they went to because it gives all kinds of revealing information. Everything from what part of the country they're from to their socioeconomic and cultural backgrounds. It's an easy way to learn a ton about a person in a short time and start a connection."

I then paused and showed Lonnie my empty martini glass. Next, with a sheepish grin, I brought it to my chin, chiming, "I'm out of gin." And, with a wink, I clinked his drink and said, "Catch you later." As I walked away, I could identify with the fact that alcohol could be used as a short-term lubricant for your frame of mind.

THOUGHTS ON PARENTING
AND LIFE OBJECTIVES

Waiting at the jam-packed bar, I spotted a stack of old Midwood newsletters. Appropriately, they were from the spring of 1962, filled with stories of students winning prizes in science, athletics, and music. As I perused an issue, an old friend, Peter Brown, walked by. Reading about exceptional talent and seeing Peter made me think of the different levels of students.

Pete was an average student who was good at track, but not Olympic material. Like most, he was talented in some areas, mediocre in many, and subpar in others; nothing remarkable about him, just an ordinary Joe. I pondered, why is there this almost obsessive propensity to become exceptional? Is "average" synonymous with a meaningless life, because extraordinary is what the public views as success? Is this one reason why many people have poor self-esteem? Parents, naturally, want their children to be happy and praise them time and again. Sometimes unrealistic expectations have ruined adults who've had rose-colored childhoods. Real life has been a rude awakening for a generation of young adults who've been told they could do anything and later discovered that often isn't true. Isn't it prudent to cultivate a truthful appreciation for whatever talents we possess? Isn't trying and accepting ourselves, for the most part, all that matters?

I'm of the opinion that harsh reality is better than false hope. We're all aware of individuals who've squandered their gifts through laziness, indifference, or greed. Do people have an obligation to live up to their potential? The question shouldn't be solely about accomplishments but what you've done with your gifts or how you've played your hand. Josh Shipp said, "You can either get bitter or get better. It's that simple. You either take what's been dealt you and allow it to make you a better person, or you allow it to tear you down. The choice doesn't belong to fate. It belongs to you." Then again, everyone knows people of differing talent levels can and do find meaning in life. These questions are way above my pay grade. Therefore, maybe we should ask psychiatrists' psychiatrists about these uncertainties.

When choosing careers or objectives in life, there are often conflicts between achievements needed for the marketplace (professional degrees, resumes) clashing with virtues you would like extolled at your very own eulogy (integrity, kindness, love, compassion, friendship).

Though society usually favors impressive resumes because they enhance our marketing, it's the nonmaterial qualities we hope are paid tribute to at our death. We recognize the virtues held in highest regard are nonmaterial, but our culture and educational system spend more time teaching skills required for career success than qualities of selflessness. "Men for the sake of getting a living forget to live" (M. Fuller).

We frequently judge people by what they did. But there are so many different considerations to measure people's worth. Were they loved, or did they love? Did they have children, grandchildren?

What were their accomplishments? Which is right? Although the two directions aren't mutually exclusive, and most of us don't have one true calling, it's always a thought-provoking and important consideration which area or path a person stresses going through life.

Talented individuals certainly stand out when demonstrating their superior skills. For the most part, they are passionate and perseverant in their endeavors, which in itself is appealing. "Whatever you are by nature, keep to it; never desert your line of talent. Be what nature intended you for and you'll succeed" (Sydney Smith). As a rule, when people practice and improve on their talents, they flourish. Be that as it may, most of us get very few exceptional gifts.

Do talent and creativity in an area (music, art, sports, cooking, or even good listening skills) make a person more attractive? Yes, because such people usually are self-assured. Confidence makes interactions with them more interesting and entertaining. As a rule, people who regard themselves well more easily gain the confidence of others.

CHINESE FOOD - AROUND THE CORONER

My heavy, thought-provoking meanderings were interrupted by a rhythmic series of thumps to the back of my shoulder. After turning quickly to identify the rapper, I racked my brain, straining to remember his name, but couldn't. I did, however, recognize the lady next to him. The thumper said, "I know I've changed a lot, but I'm John Kleindick, and this is Ling Ting Tung."

It was a gimme recalling Ling Ting Tung because there were so few Asians in our school. In fact, I remembered Miss Tung well because we were lab partners in chemistry. We sat alphabetically, but, more noteworthy, I had a crush on this newly arrived, attractive young lady from Beijing. Science labs often carried over into our lunch breaks, which, looking back, probably factored into my fling with Ling.

Customarily, once a week my family went to a Chinese restaurant. Though we usually ordered too much, doggy bagging the leftovers, they were long gone before I could even think about bringing the chow for lunch. More often than not, I purchased the school's crappy cafeteria food. Ling Ting, however, regularly brown-bagged Chinese food from her parents' new restaurant. Many times I remember asking her, "What's for lunch?" Ling Ting Tung would smile and in broken English—or maybe it was correct Chinese—say, "Egg Foo Yung." To this day I wonder if Ling Ting's lunch line was tongue in cheek.

As an aside, she was a young woman that, you could say, I was more than infatuated with. "Tung tied" would've been a better phrase, because I'd follow Ling Ting all over the place. She was pretty, bright, and showed me the way in lab and other areas. We really had good chemistry!

I had a love-hate relationship with my mother. (At the time I didn't know she was bipolar and thought she was normal.) Usually, I had a loving relationship with her, but sometimes I'd look for ways to piss off my very Jewish mother. I still remember my mother's face when I said, "I think this thing with Ling is for real. How about our family trying out her restaurant? I heard the food's great. This way our families could meet."

After going back in time recalling my love of Ling (not so lovely anymore), my thoughts now switched back to her sidekick. Again digging into my past, I still couldn't remember this vaguely familiar guy until he spoke once more. "We took science and math together." Triggered by his hoarse, guttural voice, a light bulb went on—mad scientist John Kleindick. I recalled a small, grumpy, nerdy kid who sat in the front of every class. John, I also remembered, wasn't your typical ordinary, ornery guy. He was extremely smart but totally awkward and socially out of step. Because Kleindick was such an oddball, many classmates avoided him at all costs. I also remember John constantly obsessing about things.

Always dangling from John's belt was his slide rule. I was impressed with anyone who had one but had no idea how it worked. I once borrowed his slide rule to impress Marsha, a sharp-as-a-tack, developing teen I had the hots for. Although relatively quiet, she had an incisive wit, combined with a disarming directness and assertiveness I genuinely admired. To this day, I have a weakness for this type of strong-willed woman. However, besides not knowing how the slide rule worked, I didn't have a clue how to wear it. Hanging and swaying incorrectly from my belt, the swinging slide rule kept whacking my crotch. This cracked everyone up, though the girls seemed to enjoy it more. Merely thinking about it reminds me of my feelings of humiliation and being the butt of their laughter, though it was the front of my pants. (I wonder if that's how the word "crotchety" was derived.)

After chatting for more minutes than I liked, I recognized John had physically changed but appeared nerdy as ever. Bald as a bowling ball with a scrunched-up and collapsed face, he could've passed for Popeye's clone. Adding to his comical appearance, Kleindick wore his pants ridiculously nipple high. I wasn't the least bit surprised when quirky Kleindick said, "I became a coroner after completing medical school." Also not unexpectedly, John was still passionate about numbers, because he bounced this statistic off me: "You know the cost of living is going up, but the chance of living is going down."

John, I further recall, had a morbid side (medical examiner, pathologist), which resurfaced when he said, "I haven't bought any clothes since the first President Bush. I've got bad genes and don't think I'll be around much longer. My parents and siblings are long gone." He then paused, likely for the comedic/dramatic effect— I'm not sure which one or both—and added, "I think death is just around the *coroner.*"

"That's awesome!" I said. "Loved that play on words, and that's coming from a person who's really into double entendre."

John continued his spiel: rambling on about life's certain inevitability. "Old age is regarded as unavoidable and undesirable. It's a problem-infested phase we're all compelled, or make that hope, to experience. We're all dying, just at different rates, marking our time till our final exit from life."

I winced and recoiled, then stated, "If I agreed with you, we'd both be wrong. I don't think old age is a grim time you have to somehow endure and make the best of, but a time of leisure and freedom to explore whatever you wish. Though the marks of breakdown are all too visible, perhaps, with a little luck, we'll live more or less intact another decade and be granted the good fortune to be appreciated. I don't feel I have one foot in the grave. I have a broader perspective of life."

Nevertheless, Kleindick relentlessly continued. "I've bought my last car, pair of shoes, and whatever. Now I enjoy giving things away. Hey, you look about my size; do you want any of my clothes?"

Getting more depressed by the minute and not knowing what to say, I thought, "Intellectual brilliance is no guarantee of being dead wrong." On the other hand, I did consider his clothing offer, as I get a kick out of wearing hand-me-downs. I said to John, "I could use a blue blazer like yours." But, as I got closer to it, there definitely was a foul odor emanating from it. Therefore, I didn't think I'd smell top-notch in Kleindick's formaldehyde-laden jacket. Touching his lapel and then placing my fingers to my nose, I wisecracked, "I think I'll pass on your sports jacket. In the past you've got too close to those who've passed." Immediately, I realized my attempt to say something serious through humor came up short. Though, as we often look back on things we've said, on the spur of the moment, that's what I came up with.

Considering another drink but knowing I'd be driving home in an hour, I vetoed the notion. After leaving John and while roaming among the throngs of mostly unknown classmates, I thought of Oscar Wilde's line, "Some cause happiness wherever they go, others whenever they go." Following some deep breaths, I felt relieved escaping from that depressing, almost-dead nerd-geek, or whatever you want to call him.

DRUGS KEEP US GOING

B y chance, as I strolled out of the ballroom to get some water, I ran into a long-ago friend, Herb Stein, still looking like the tall drink of water of yesteryear, also leaving the room. As I was about to say hello, I couldn't help but notice Herb pulling a plastic pillbox from his sports coat. "Great to see ya—any good Herb-al medicines in there for me?" I bantered.

Grinning broadly, Herb replied, "How've ya been, Ron? I've gotta take more blood pressure pills, now at night, in addition to all the other shit I take. Any idea where's the water fountain?"

"Not a clue; let's go look," I said.

As we walked, I mused, "Every time I go to a doctor, I wind up taking more pills. I take a lot—mostly in the morning. Lately, I'm tempted to dump them all in a bowl, put some ketchup on them, and that'll be breakfast."

Upon locating the water fountain, I continued, "Boy, am I thirsty. Had a few drinks tonight; that probably did it. Talking about drinks, I'm sure you've heard most doctors allow their patients to have a drink a day? Fortunately for me, I have five doctors!"

At the water fountain, Herb and I were warmly greeted by a former friend, Andy Wasserman, or Wass, as we called him. Both Herb and I practically competed to give him our days-of-old Midwood greeting: "What's up, Wass?" Furthermore, the two of us were not surprised that Andy was also downing some pills but were completely shocked to see how heavy he had gotten.

After weighing Andy in on our pill-popping discussion, Herb said, "I'm sick and tired of going to doctors and taking all these damn pills. They control my life. When I think about all the time I go to physicians, sit in their waiting rooms, and the never-ending follow-up visits! Then I gotta drive to the pharmacy, sort the morning and night pills, try to figure which meds need water, which need food, load my mammoth pillbox, and finally gulp them down. Lately, I've been thinking—FUKITOL!"

Quickly looking at Wass's flabbergasted, opened-mouth expression and then at Herb, I said, "You're not serious, are ya, Herb?" I asked in disbelief, although I did remember Herb liked to pull a leg now and then.

"No, not at all, but that's how I remember all these fuckin' pills. F is for my heart fibrillations, U—ulcers, K__ kidney stones, I—irritable bowel, T—thyroid, etc." Kibitzing around some more, he continued, "By the way, guys, I learned something from my internist that's extremely important. Make sure you know your pill's purpose, since it's possible to take a sleeping pill and a laxative the same night!" (Though the joke was as old as the people in attendance, Wass and I just looked at each other and smirked, never telling Herb we've heard it more than once before.)

Relieved, realizing Herb was just kidding, Andy and I beamed, thoroughly appreciating his on-the-money pill parody. Be that as it may and not to be outdone, Wass enlightened us as to his massive size by giving us the lowdown on his weight gain, disclosing, "I also just went to the doctor, and, like both of you, he increased my meds. Now I'm taking ten pills, or it might even be eleven. Only problem—most of the pills I take have a warning, 'Must be taken with food'! So now you know why I'm over three hundred pounds and climbing! Know what I'm doing next week? Looking for a doctor who specializes in dieting! Unfortunately, I'm sure it'll mean taking some more pills."

TEEN AWAKENINGS

Not surprisingly, as I wandered about, I recognized more of the men than the women. The reason is that during our early schooling, most of us were considerably more comfortable with kids of our own gender. Teleologically (the purpose and design of nature), especially through puberty, it certainly seemed commonsensical to keep the sexes apart, otherwise not much would get done. During adolescence, due to our rising testosterone, most males' thoughts fixated on sex. I believe most guys felt pangs of shame feeling this way, yet in the grand design, I think it was purposeful. Though these levels declined and then dwindled with advancing years, these early feelings influenced a good number of men's relationships with women throughout life.

Returning to the ballroom, I again encountered the familiar grin of Laura Salmon (reunion chairperson) as she talked to some woman I didn't recognize. "What's the smile about?" I asked.

"Ron, you remember Ginger Starr?" I never would've recognized this attractive woman, but the name certainly conjured up, as if it were yesterday, the stunning redhead who, during my sexual awakenings, more than stirred my anatomy. Thinking back, I easily recalled this never-to-be-forgotten ripening teenager. I also remembered just about every teenage guy's eyes secretly following her around similarly. Come to think of it, many of the guys' looks weren't so furtive at all. Now, hoping the two couldn't read my thoughts, I responded by nodding yes, desperately hoping Ginger wouldn't remember me.

Midwood, like every Brooklyn high school, was where they threw thousands of pubescent male teenagers in a coed school and assumed they wouldn't be thinking about sex (maybe for fifteen seconds). In actuality, for my friends, Hormonal High would've been a more appropriate name for our high school—or make that probably any high school.

Ginger, at the time of my heightening sexuality, was one of the first to blossom. It was late spring, with temperatures and other things rising, when my discerning eyes couldn't help notice this well-endowed, maturing teen looking better and better every day. Sitting diagonally behind her, I was mesmerized by her clinging, voluptuous appendages. It looked as if every fiber of each outfit she wore strained to contain her assets. Unfortunately for me and many guys, Ginger seemed to have eyes in the back of her head, detecting our yearning adolescent cravings. For sure, she constantly caught this guy.

I was precocious and oversexed (though thinking back, it's hard to measure how my motor compared to others) and recall feasting my eyes on her even before my bar mitzvah, the age you're supposed to become a man. At that ungainly age, still a boy but longing to be older, I remember hanging out with my horny pals and remember one of them bullshitting, "A girl is said to be grown when she starts wearing a bra. I wonder if a boy is considered grown when he starts removing it?"

Eventually, I mustered the courage to ask her out and was quite shocked that she agreed. Of course, for the week before, I was a nervous wreck. On the night of the date, I distinctly recall sweating profusely as I readied to ring Ginger's doorbell. I'll also never forget thinking, even her doorbell looked like a miniature breast. Always feeling more demented than most, I gently pushed the nipple and waited, hoping this would be my lucky day and that our relationship would flower.

FYI, and without getting into details, we were only breast friends for a short time. However, what ecstasy! Ginger taught this blundering, inexperienced teenager lessons that lessened the need for me to take more lessons for quite a while. Regrettably, however, Ginger soon found other interests. And whenever we passed in the hallways, she gave me the cold shoulder, leaving no ifs, ands, or butts about it.

At the reunion, I found it especially ironic that seeing Ginger prompted the memories of my surging teenage hormones, which now sharply contrast with my petering eighth-decade testosterone levels. Like most of us there that night, my once effective erogenous zone had to some extent slumped.

Digressing for a moment, back then, didn't most teens assume their friends were having sex, even though we ourselves weren't? And now, fifty years later, do most seniors think their peers are having it?

Laura Salmon interrupted my musings, saying, "Ron, I was smiling because Ginger revealed a couple of things that were really perceptive. Things I've never heard expressed before. She said she feels old because many of her doctors are our peers and they're retiring also. So now she's looking for new ones." I readily smiled, knowing it to be so true. "Ron, she also told me that as a teenager, whenever she had a bad hair day, her solution was to wear a low-cut blouse."

After Ginger's disclosure, I just couldn't help myself (I'm sure other readers would be interested too) and peeked at her décolletage, where a long, gold locket nestled in the gully between her still-ample twin peaks, went south, and disappeared. (I might've gotten away with it.) At that moment, I thought, "Lucky new doctors, and thanks for the mammaries!"

SURROGATE PARENTS

I did an about-face when I noticed Gary Harrison, a friend I hadn't seen in a couple of years, dash across the ballroom and just about jump into my arms. As we bear-hugged and clapped each other on the back on the dance floor, he excitedly said, "So glad to see ya! I bet a lot of guys freaked out when they saw you here." Gary couldn't stop smiling, his face lighting up like an ecstatic child.

"It's Harry Garrison!" I said, using the flip-flopped name I often called him as kids. Harry (who rarely was harried) and I met in kindergarten and attended every school together, even college and Hebrew. Gary and I, or Mutt and Jeff, as we were also known, were joined at the hip and stayed lifelong friends. As kids, we played every schoolyard game and slept at each other's houses.

Play, by the way, is often talked about as if it were a relief from serious-minded learning. But for children, it is serious learning in many ways. Play is also like sleep. You need it to recharge for creativity or work. It's a necessity at any age and one of the reasons I write. I can play on a page like a child left alone on a beach to have fun with sand. Originally, Gary and our third Musketeer, Michael Kramer (hooked up in third grade), became friends through play. To this day, we still make merry, carouse, or whatever you want to call it in an assortment of ways. It is one of the many reasons why we've remained lifelong friends.

Harry/Gary was the last of my peers to have both parents alive. Gary's mother and father were almost surrogate parents to me. Fannie and Nate came to my rescue many a time, as my manic-depressive mother, with a mixed record in being a model mother, was normally off the wall. No one in my family escaped unscathed. As kids, my sisters and I lived in a state of near permanent anxiety resulting from her handicap. My father always worked and was never available.

The presence of strangers was the only guarantee of good behavior from my mother. As a kid, I can't tell you how many times friends came over for salami sandwiches. As a young teenager, and not knowing her problem or what was normal, I'd inwardly get a kick out of pushing her buttons on an almost daily basis. They say the troublesome ones in a family are usually either the wits or idiots. I was talented; I starred in both roles. Looking back, as I said, she was bipolar, but when I made the scene, she often made a scene and became tripolar.

Contributing to our tempestuous relationship were the many stories I told. As a kid I lied a lot. My mother caught me loads of times, which resulted in me leading my neighborhood in punishments. As a fortuitous consequence of my untruths, she gave me words of wisdom I used through life: "A liar needs a good memory" (Quintilian).

Developing a good memory came easy. Throughout my schooling, if I read and didn't understand a concept, I'd commit the page to memory. Vocabulary—no problem. As a matter of fact, in dentistry I capitalized on this gift by recalling patients' mouths, x-rays, and so on. When a patient phoned with a problem, my photodontic (no such word yet) ability could time and again pinpoint the offending tooth. This gift made patients feel special. Incidentally, after I fine-tuned this talent, my mother had a tough time figuring out which stories were real.

Though my mother was there all the time and loved and tried in her own way, maternal deprivation played a significant component in my upbringing. Therefore, the dubious haven of home or family was never part of my mind-set or upbringing.

Going off on a tangent once more, to this day, my wife, the person I listen to most, has expressed a point of view that might make you look at my writings differently. She has stated, "He really does have an amazing memory, but at times he can recall things that never happened."

Truth be told, there are two females to whom I listen. My wife, Iris, as mentioned, and Apple's voice-activated intelligence assistant, Siri. Now and then I've wondered if a decision maker from Apple's hierarchy is familiar with my wife's intellect, because if that person heard Iris's answers to some of the gazillion questions I've asked her over time, it may have influenced their choosing her as their role model—Iris spelled backwards is Siri!

Returning to the subject of Gary's mom and dad, I asked with trepidation, "How are your parents doing?"

"They're pretty good, considering," he answered. "Funny you should ask. Next week we're celebrating their seventieth anniversary. My father is ninety-three and Fannie ninety. They're both somewhat frail, as you'd expect; live in an assisted-living facility; and, amazingly, still fight every day. Please come! They'd love to see you. It's right here on Long Island—only family. No friends, they're all gone. One by one their friends became homebound, bedridden, lost their minds, or died. It's sad and certainly ironic; they've won the longevity game but lost every friend along the way. Everyone wants long life, but no one wants to grow old and have no friends."

"Wow, seventieth anniversary—that's amazing!" I said. "Speaking of seventy, did you know someone told me at the reunion tonight that in a few years they're planning our seventieth anniversary from kindergarten?

"No way—you're kidding, right? Gary questioned.

"No, it's really true. Can you imagine someone recognizing me? I'm worried about the hundred and seventy-five pounds I've gained since then," I deadpanned. Watching Gary grin from ear to ear brought me back to the days of yore, when we laughed about everything in sight, or so it seemed.

Getting back to his parents, Gary said, "At times, my father still knocks me for a loop. The other day he said, 'Growing old is basically a process of watching everything you know in the world disappear. Live long enough, and the world starts becoming an unrecognizable place.'

"That's some pretty heavy thoughts. I'm amazed he's still so sharp. I'll never forget the joke he told to us as teens in the carpet and linoleum store your family owned in our neighborhood. Does he still have his great sense of humor?" I inquired.

"Which joke? He had lots," Gary asked.

Fielding the question with a smirk, I said, "The one about women and linoleum floors. He said, 'Lay 'em right, and for thirty years you can walk all over them.'"

Gary smiled and proudly revealed, "Surprisingly, my father never lost his sense of humor, although in other ways he's certainly losing it. The other day he clowned, 'You know the best thing about being a nonagenarian (ninety years old)? No peer pressure! As a matter of fact, the line about respecting your elders can be kissed good-bye too.'"

"You gotta come see them; bring Iris," Gary pleaded.

"For sure, can't wait," I said without batting an eye. "This way we'll catch up in a calmer setting. We've got lots to talk about. Tonight there's still a ton of people we both want to see. See ya next week. By the way, look who just came."

THE SCHLEPS SCHLEP IN

Making their entrance were the Schlepowitz twins. They were among the weirdest dudes in our neighborhood. That was quite a distinction; tells you an awful lot how screwed up they were. Our stomping grounds might've led the borough in crazy loons. Frank and Lester were identical, and I'm not proud to say they are my distant cousins. Of course, everyone called them the Schleps. Both were not much to look at, frightfully thin, and cross eyed, and one lisped. They were bright enough, average athletes whom you couldn't possibly tell apart, except for the lisp. I always tried to figure out which eye they focused with and not get caught staring, but never could. Surprisingly, that night they looked much better than in high school. Each had gained weight, had his eyes fixed, and had more hair than most, but still looked and acted like a schlep.

On the positive side, they were always fun, easy to goof with, and totally frank. Lester was less frank than Frank, or, clearing it up, Frank was more frank. To this day I've never seen two guys put down and humiliate each other as well as they did! The twins took turns as stooges, setting the other up for remarks that were so cutting that they went beyond outrageous! What made it funnier was that their wit always had some truth to it. They loved the rough-and-ready exchange of banter and were always on. Show time—first one, then the other! They operated on a different fuel mixture than most, constantly making their friends smile ear to ear. That night as I listened to them hold court in front of a dozen or so classmates, I learned they were retired elementary school teachers who never married. Les added, "We live in Florida, where, as it's said, the temperature never goes below your age. Golf and play the horses almost every day."

After their performance broke up, I gave them a warm hello. "I'm surprised to see ya, Ron, since you never graduated," the better-looking Schlep said.

After schmoozing for a while, I said, "Do you remember my uncle Meyer Sobotkin, the New York City cop? He just died. In fact, I think he was related to you two."

Les Schlepowitz lisped (or was it Frank? I forgot who was who), "Yes, he was, and of course I do. He was one tough cookie. Took no shit from anyone. That's too bad, but I'm sure he was way up there, age wise."

I told whichever Schlep, "He said something to me before he died I'll never forget."

"What's that?" whichever one of them asked.

"Two or three years before he died, Uncle Meyer lost his daughter and wife. Now wearing Coke-bottle glasses, going blind, he said, 'If you think life is tough now—just wait, just wait. All the problems you've had so far won't come close to preparing you for the things to come.'"

Shaking his head, the more unappealing Schlep said in a not-too-articulate manner, "Fuckin' unbelievable! I gotta get me a drink."

As the twins and I walked over to the bar, Les, who lisped less than I recall, stopped unexpectedly by a woman who had gained more than a few pounds—"ballooned" might've been a better word—and bellowed, "I didn't exthpect anyone from our clath to be pregnant!" Both Schleps doubled over in laughter; Les's words caused everyone to cringe and look away. Adding to the embarrassment, the Schleps' trademark loud, cackling, machine-gun-like laughter, over and above, hit the victims like a ton of bricks.

After Lester quickly downed his martini, he moseyed over to the piano lounge, where a handful of coed classmates were kibitzing. Shortly thereafter, he tried to hit on a short, thin woman, whose back was toward him. Getting nowhere, he dispiritedly asked the bartender for another drink. While waiting, his brother came next to him and ordered a scotch. Les turned to Frank and said, "Ithn't that a beautiful rosthe on the piano?"

Frank, always being frank in speaking what he thought, glared at Les and exclaimed, "When do you ever notice a rose on a piano?"

Les responded, fighting to hold back his smile, which ultimately he could not. "You know the only thing better than a rosthe on a piano? Two lipths on an organ."

The woman Les tried to hit on, overhearing what was said, turned sharply to face him. With drink in hand, looking like she felt no pain, pretending to be horrified, she said, "That's disgusting, but I loved it! Wait till my friends at the Bristol assisted living hear it. They'll crack up. By the way, following up on that, back then, my favorite song was "The Happy Organ" by Dave Baby Cortez." She paused for a few seconds and then, realizing what she said, turned beet red. Almost whispering, she added, "If you see my son, Lonnie, don't tell him I said that—or, for that matter, don't tell anyone else, either."

After Les recognized his ninety-plus-year-old former math teacher, Mrs. Kaufman, he also turned red, thoroughly embarrassed! Trying to be less of a schlep, but still blowing it, he said, "I'm really shocked to see you. From the *angle* where I was sitting, you look half your age. You really have *acute* figure and not a bad *set*. See, I still remember some of the math terms you taught me. Can I buy you another drink? Again, I'm really sorry."

After finishing his whatever number martini, Les Schlep blabbered, "Even though I'd like another drink, Mrs. K, my plumbing is killing me. I gotta go. But before I do, I gotta tell ya about my urologist. Yesterday, when I was there, his waiting room was filled with all over-eighty-five-year-old men. I thought I was at a reunion there, too—only this time, it looked like a reunion for Civil War veterans." Always loving his own sense of humor, his machine-gun laughter stridently rat-a-tatted again, cracking himself up. This in turn made his comical face even more absurd.

Suddenly, Les experienced a violent spasm of pain. Grimacing, he lisped to Mrs. K, "Ya know, when you have a bladder problem, urine trouble. Any idea where's the bathrooms?"

Have you noticed, or is it just me, some people with lots of mileage on them become looser lipped and speak out tactlessly? Similar to individuals challenged with Asperger's syndrome, a number of seniors lose their inhibitory abilities or filtering mechanisms. They don't realize they're being rude when they express things undiplomatically, thoughts that shouldn't be voiced out loud. Hippel University of Wales, Australia, confirmed, "The aging brain changes, while not necessarily affecting intelligence, but can affect other mental functions like inhibition. Older adults, still sharp as a tack, may say things that embarrass us without intending to do so." For this reason, I beg the question—is it by design that nature wants us to tell it like it is very late in life, or is it built into the system to depart this world before we lose our filtering processes?

After considering that the bungling Schleps weren't born with too many filters to begin with, and upon hearing the twins carry on with their fellow alumni, it was obvious the few they have left were diminishing. Given that I'm a distant cousin, I'm more than concerned this shortcoming might raise its ugly head in my lifetime.

109

NEIGHBORHOOD'S TOP BANANA

Near the piano, getting a kick out of the Schleps' shticks, was a smiling Bob Salerno. Salerno was not your typical school-mate with a good sense of humor. Bob was a free-as-the-wind, spontaneous, intelligent guy who laughed at the absurdities of ev-eryday life. He was also down to earth and had impeccable tim-ing. "I love people who make me laugh. I think it's the thing I like most, to laugh. It cures a multitude of ills. It's probably the most important thing in a person" (Audrey Hepburn). Most people rec-ognized Bob's uniqueness the instant they met. They knew meet-ing a person like him, if they were lucky, only happens a few times. Bob's demeanor shone in the grays of life. He carried himself, in both manner and originality, like a movie star. In any crowd he stood out, drawing every person's eyes. He was part of our circle of friends who, in my opinion could've made it in stand-up comedy. He delivered the kind of humor that made you laugh for five sec-onds and then think about it for ten minutes.

Bob was the best in a neighborhood chock full of comedians, adopting a Robin Williamsesque style before there was a Robin Williams. A number of classmates begged him to give his take on being a senior. Obligingly, he transported us back in time to our old stomping grounds, as he spewed forth in rapid-fire Brooklynese.

With drink in hand, Salerno extemporaneously hit the ground running, holding court to a dozen or so classmates. Pointing to the area below his belt, Bob said, "All major decisions in life are made in this area. When you're young, you spend all your time contemplating making love." Appropriately, using Robin Williams line, Salerno said, 'God gives man a brain and penis, and only enough blood to run one at a time.'"

After the laughter subsided, he continued, "As you age, your entire life is controlled by the bathroom. The symptoms are nearly identical: constant focus and strong urges every five minutes. At this age, it's a necessity to know where the nearest bathroom is at all times." Salerno took out his iPhone and, while pointing to it, said, "I've downloaded the app Toilet Finder, which pinpoints where you are in relation to the closest bathroom." As I scanned the group, everyone was beaming.

"Most of you don't know this, but I'm now temporarily in a rehab facility. This time it's due to recent knee replacement, which, as you well know, comes with the territory. Incidentally, at my first postsurgical visit, I told my orthopedist, 'I feel fine, but I think I have fluid on my knee.'

"After the doctor thoroughly examined my knee, he said, 'You're fine. You're just not aiming right!'"

After the chuckling died down, Bob went on. "Now that my knee has healed, I'm attempting things no person in our age bracket should ever try. I'm practicing senior pole dancing, without the pole. Fortunately, for the well-being of the rehab residents, everyone who participates must hold on to a bathroom safety bar. Surprisingly, at some assisted living facilities, they're having competitions in this burlesque-like activity." Bob then brought the house down by pretending to disrobe and prance about erotically. Following the raucous laughter, he finished with, "Now this silver fox is thinking about a new career. After I gulp down a few Viagra and Cialis, I'm practicing to become a senior porn star. By the way, ironically, my first wife's name was Alice. But believe me, if the manufacturers ever saw her, they'd never name an erection enhancer after her. Now getting back to my new pursuit, just imagine me all decked out, entering some old-age home, warning the women, 'Be careful, ladies, watch out, watch out, I don't want any of you to get hurt!'"

"You don't stop laughing because you grow old. You grow old because you stop laughing." (M. Pritchard).

AMBULANCE TO THE RESCUE

Listening as well to this was way-out, weird Woody Brill, a difficult guy to explain. He was bright, unpredictably nuts, hotheaded, and lived every day as if it was Saturday night. What's more, he never lost his temper; he took it with him at all times. He was also fond of taking a stab at anything. As a matter of fact, I'll never forget the time an oversized football player pissed him off, and Woody warned, "There's a butcher's knife waiting for your heart if you try that again." After an intense faceoff, the Goliath, evidently realizing Brill was crazed beyond all reason, meekly walked away.

Be that as it may, every person who made contact with him had great difficulty deciphering what the hell he was talking about. Many times I gave him my full concentration, trying to figure out his gobbledygook, but couldn't. He brought speaking gibberish to an art form. People who tried to understand him thought there was something wrong with themselves. If I tried, I couldn't speak well enough to be as unintelligible as Woody.

Our wives met at a charity event, not knowing their husbands were in the same high school graduating class. The ladies shared many interests, including tennis, golf, and art projects. They spent lots of time together and became friends. We didn't. I became anxious every double date because I got stuck listening to his mumbo-jumbo.

The Brills lived in Huntington, New York, an hour's drive from the large lumber yard Woody owned in Queens (fitting vocational name). He had amazing hands. He could build and fix anything, even cars, which certainly was an anomaly for any Jewish kid I've ever known.

Woody loved David Letterman's *Late Show* and was an avid NASCAR enthusiast. Because of his grueling physical work and TV watching, Woody overslept many times. Consequently, time and again he raced to work on the Long Island Expressway and received a slew of speeding tickets. This mandated the DMV to revoke his driver's license. With that in mind, what could he do?

Woody, always thinking outside the box, purchased a used ambulance to get to work. He figured no one would question an ambulance's speed. He also loved showing it off and brought the vehicle to our house for a spin. To say we were stunned when he pulled into our driveway, sirens wailing, would be a gross understatement. What's more, he took our young sons for an unforgettable ride.

Scott, our oldest, recalls, "I'll always remember the surreal feeling of being inside and the shocked faces of the neighbors. Surprisingly, when I lay on the mattress, it was more comfortable than I expected. It certainly was strange going ninety miles per hour with those ear-piercing sirens blasting."

For your information, in the years he drove the ambulance illegally, Woody never got caught driving without a license, nor even pulled over. Eventually, he did pay the fines and passed the road test. However, to this day, I am somewhat surprised he didn't use his ambulance to retake the test.

Fast forward twenty-five years to south Florida, where my wife and I are semiretired and winter. Recently, the Brills gave us the honor of visiting, which I sweated, the reason being that even though I didn't want to, I knew I wouldn't be able to help myself, and, while listening to Woody, I'd attempt to decode his gibberish again. For dinner, Woody and I went to pick up Italian takeout food. On the way back, my wife phoned, asking us to pick up soda. Wanting to get back ASAP, we pulled into a CVS, the most convenient store along the way. We were hungry and didn't want the food to get cold.

Unfortunately, there were about a dozen people ahead of us and only one cashier. She looked maybe fourteen. The cashier was in the midst of checking out an extremely hard-of-hearing, ninety-year-old-looking lady. Besides struggling to hear, the old woman couldn't see. The cashier, at full volume, yelled, "That's not a nickel you're giving me from your purse, ma'am. That's a battery, and it's probably for your hearing aids. Maybe that's why you're having trouble hearing."

Woody and I looked at each other and snickered, loving the cashier's commentary. Getting more impatient, Woody said, "This is ridiculous. We gotta get out of here. Listen, after I do my thing, rush to the front of the line, pay for the sodas, and head out the door."

Because—I'm not proud to say—we both had had a couple of drinks before we left the house, and because I knew of Woody's past pranks, I knew this could be interesting.

Woody then proceeded to feign a heart attack. He started moaning, grabbed his chest, and, in slow motion, fell. With Woody down for the count, pretending to have passed out, customers were flabbergasted and scared to death. I yelled, "Call 9-1-1! Could someone please call 9-1-1."

In the turmoil, I ran to the head of the line and told the cashier, who was transfixed watching the medical emergency, "Could you ring me up? I just want to pay and get out of here."

Predictably flustered, the very young teenager said, "But sir, someone's having a heart attack. We must take care of him first."

I said, "What's the difference? You've gotta wait for the ambulance anyway. Just let me pay."

And she did.

After I paid, Woody jumped up and, while brushing himself off, started for the door. While waiting for him, I couldn't help but notice the patrons, with wide-open mouths, staring in disbelief. They were shell shocked, not believing what they witnessed, especially when they watched us giving each other over-the-top, histrionic high fives. To this day I'm not sure if anyone called for an ambulance.

WINDING DOWN

I enjoyed the reunion on many levels, but unfortunately time zoomed by, and, in a blink of an eye, the night was over. Looking back, I wasn't totally surprised that it was a night when everybody showed up old but grew younger as the night went on. It was comforting being around classmates who shared, more or less, the same experiences in time and place as me. In some ways, these classmates were extensions of my immediate family.

The past influences our personality. Therefore, to what degree are we shaped by our childhoods? Can we circumvent the influence of our past? Psychiatrists say we cannot. Sure, the period of being young represents innocence, but it also might contain the key to decoding our adult makeup. Naturally, a half century later, faces and places from bygone days are more than somewhat hazy.

I believe one of the purposes of life is to accumulate memories. Our lives are the culmination of all these moments, and, in the end, that's all we have. After saying my *heartfelt farewells*, fitting portmanteaus (words formed by the merging of other words), it was uncomfortable thinking I'd never see most of them again.

"Every parting is like a form of death." (Edwards). I hate the afore-mentioned good-byes. There seems to be so many these days.

As time goes by, I'm committing my thoughts to paper because I'm more than aware of the fleeting nature of life. M. Richler said, "To counteract dying, the permanence of written words will live on." Ben Franklin also recognized the fundamental desire for self-commemoration when he wrote so eloquently, "If you would not be forgotten as soon as you are dead, either write things worth reading, or do things worth writing."

Serendipitously, I've chosen a career in dentistry, which allows me to live on for a little longer after I've passed. I've created, like countless dentists before me, functional restorations that could last thirty years or more after I'm pushing up daisies. Consequently, through dentistry, my time on earth will be prolonged.

Rabbi H. Kushner might have said it best: "I'm convinced, it's not the fear of death that haunts our sleep so much as the fear that as far as the world is concerned, we may as well never have lived."

Like many of my gray peers living in their golden years have learned, the wisdom attributed to old age is wildly overrated. I suspected this when younger but had to age to confirm it. Pretty much everyone wings it; some simply do it better and more confi-dently. At times, I still feel childlike when major difficulties arise. Life is full of problem solving, which at any age can be daunting. Each phase, as you know, has its own new and unique problems. Without predicaments you wouldn't be alive. Frequently, you're not sure how to deal with these quandaries, but they sure make life interesting. On the other hand, Oscar Wilde's line "I'm not young enough to know everything" did cross my mind.

Nevertheless, worrying about tomorrow's unknown troubles takes away from today's peace. A fitting anecdote: A man ninety years old was asked what he attributed his longevity to. He said, with a twinkle in his eye, "It's because most nights I went to bed and slept when I should have sat up and worried" (Dorothea Kent).

Therefore, chill out, don't spend too much time worrying about what might happen, much of which will never transpire. One day your heart will stop, and none of your fears will matter. What matters is how you lived.

K. Pillemer, Cornell University, confirmed the number one regret of people nearing death is wishing they spent less time worrying. Kristen Wong's research, "The Biggest Wastes of Time We Regret When We Get Older," added that not asking for help, trying to make bad relationships work, dwelling on mistakes and shortcomings, and worrying too much about other people were listed as additional culprits.

Be that as it may, in spite of everything my peer group has experienced, I'm well aware heavy weather lies ahead. Therefore, as the number of my tomorrows dwindles, I'm hoping to make a concerted effort to savor each moment. One day the present will be a distant memory for which we'll yearn. Go for it now. The future is promised to no one.

Some friends were chagrined I wrote a great deal about darkness and the deep troubles that go along with aging. Throughout our lives, we have to confront many things we would rather not experience but can't do anything about.

I think of death. Nothing crazy; I don't obsess, but it's on my mind. I feel vulnerable; I'm human. I don't know what other people think, but I imagine many elderly do think deeply about it. You're off your rocker, at this point in time, if you don't.

Thinking about death is natural when it's done inwardly, to enhance your self-awareness of what you'd like to accomplish with the time you have left. You should think about priorities. I don't feel I'm overthinking death, but, as Vin Scully said, "You can't push the setting sun back in the sky."

We oldies continually talk to each other about the inconveniences of aging and endlessly compare our pathologies and prostheses. We never talk about our own deaths, only those of relatives and acquaintances. I cannot pretend I am without fear. Death is not in our hands, nor do we have any control of it. Or are we all experts on death, though we know so little about it or haven't experienced it as yet? Why don't people talk about it more? Is it because talking about death is boring, since there's nothing new or interesting to say about it? I guess it's just easier to bury it God knows where; maybe put it on the back burner, as we do with so many things.

GETTING MY CAR AND DRIVING HOME

W hile I waited for the valet to get my car, loud claps of thunder, warning of an imminent downpour, interrupted my reverie. I remember thinking how glad I was somebody was getting my car in this huge parking lot, especially with this ominous weather. In the past, more than a few times, I vividly recall spending an inordinate amount of time going up and down aisles searching for my car. Given that seniors frequently have physical handicaps, are slowed by age, or have memory hiccups, wouldn't it be preferred and practical to have their vehicles retrieved by valets? After tipping the valet, I thought I'd use the hour's drive home to pore over the evening's events.

I was blown away by the celebration, which went by like a bolt of lightning, and thunderstruck by the sheer emotions of revisiting old friends. The reunion already seemed like a timeless dream. They say in extreme moments, time goes by in slow motion. Tonight, some of those everlasting images with my no-spring-chickens classmates were already being imprinted in my memory bank. How often does one recognize memories developing while the actual milestone unfolds? Almost never. I was extremely excited to tell Iris about my fiftieth and eager to hear about hers.

"Life's journey is best measured in friends, rather than miles" (Tim Cahill). In reality, all a person has is family and friends. Because man is a social creature in constant need of others, he was never meant to live by himself. "Good social relationships keep us happier and healthier, even allowing us to live longer" (R. Waldinger). Lee Iacocca's father said, "Because few things in life equal the gift of friendship, when you die, if you've had five real friends, then you had a great life." After meeting up with old pals once more, I certainly understood why rekindled friendships, with their vast histories, could burn so brightly. Consequently, the loss of any treasured friend is traumatic. In spite of this, friends come and go throughout our journeys. For this reason, it's imperative to try to make new ones.

Both our sons will be intrigued by our stories, given they recently (two years apart) celebrated their twenty-fifth reunions, though I wonder if they question, "Can parents, who are so old to every generation, possibly have that much fun at their half-century reunion?" My wife's encounter with her first boyfriend, I'm sure, will pique their interest. I'm also curious if they envision what their fiftieth might be like. Do they even wonder, God forbid, whether they will make it to their own fiftieth?

Zooming in on my sons, Scott and Eric, I wonder if it's hit them how swiftly life goes by. Or, as it often happens, are they so furiously working, raising families, and just getting through the day that it doesn't cross their minds? Day in and day out, this mad treadmill is everywhere about them. I'm sure they sense it, but it seems like a characteristic of our times never to mention it, never admit it, even to themselves. My gut feeling is that they do think about it but ever so rarely. Another folly of youth? Or is it part of nature's grand design not to think how harried the days are or how fast life gallops by?

Strange, even now, when I think of my kids and wife—though I know they're all getting older—there's a timelessness about them. It's as if their lives are happening in an ageless dream, where growing old stops when I think about them. I think we like to see our children as we wish, not as they are. Do strong bonds of love and devotion contribute to this agelessness?

Everyone remembers the neighborhood kids they grew up with. That's why high school reunions are so special. The fiftieth in particular perhaps prompts the realization—this probably will be our last chance to get together. Reunions are part of life's passages and call attention to the relentless progression of time. It seems like I had been young only a moment ago. Fiftieth reunions aren't new. They've been celebrated for decades, by small numbers at first and larger numbers later, as people live longer. For these reasons, people are more likely to attend their fiftieth, even if they've never been to a reunion before.

Back in time, I vividly recall coming across fiftieth-reunion class photos, thinking how dreadful, or predead, these barely alive people looked. Didn't you? Does my family now put me into this same category? What are my kids' thoughts on their parents becoming seventy? Some say seventy is the new fifty. With the continuous advances in medicine, I'm sure there's some truth to this. But somehow I can't help thinking, is this also a tease designed to prevent us from accepting reality? As the hands of time keep ticking at my back, one day I'll be a memory. I'm trying to be a good one.

Growing up, I never dwelled on life expectancies, although I always wanted to make it to 2000. My father died when he was exactly two thirds of a century and Mom at a pair of sevens. I'm sure, because our parents' life spans were less than ours, they thought about longevity and death, but just a little earlier. Now, when I have so many years to look back on, rather than forward, I realize many decades ago I was just naïve and oblivious to my parents' thoughts of their time on earth.

"The way to love anything is to realize that it might be lost." (Chatterton). Hate the thought, but really like what it says.

My wife was home when I pulled into the driveway. She excitedly wanted to know what transpired but also was chomping at the bit for the floor. Besides her enjoyment of meeting old friends (literally and figuratively), I knew after all these years that she looked forward to seeing her ex-boyfriend. I came along in the fall of our sophomore year in Buffalo, where we went to college, and immediately went bonkers over her. While on the subject, I've always been known to show an absence of moderation in the pursuit of my passions.

Over the years, Iris heard her old flame had done very well academically and professionally. After earning his medical degree, he worked for the World Health Organization in Switzerland. Presently, he's a dean at Duke's medical school. She also discovered he had divorced.

Regrettably, I don't have my wife's permission to put her words in writing. Her chronicles would've taken pages and been painted possibly in a measured manner. Yes, after all these years, this writer has a touch of rivalry—or make that jealousy. Although we often think of jealousy as a negative, it's really the love of our lover we're afraid of losing. This dread reminds us how much we love and need our partner. Despite what others may say, a touch of jealousy is healthy. Without leaving you hanging, I'll depart with this thought. I changed my e-mail address from sillysal to sorrysal@ optonline.net. Just kidding! Furthermore, we're approaching our fiftieth wedding anniversary, and as far as I know, it's still on.

As my candle grows shorter, I wonder at times about the raison d'être of my Midwood escapades. Was it fate that led me down the path to the University of Buffalo? Some people theorize, "Things happen for a reason." Not sure, but I never would've met my wife, which was the best thing that ever happened to me, and my life never would've turned out the way it did if I hadn't gotten arrested. Sometimes, it's been said, the best gain is to lose (George Herbert). They also say what makes people ashamed usually makes a good story.

As a result of my expulsion, I became obsessed to prove this deviant episode was a one-time screw-up. For this reason, and from that time on, I resolved to literally follow the straight and narrow, never veering off again. In addition, I felt by reaching my goals, this might soften the many hurts I caused to family and friends. I became more than willing to sacrifice a number of years, like many people won't or can't, so I could spend the rest of my life reaping the dividends of studying hard after the Midwood fiasco.

Sometimes when I look back, I think my arrest had no real purpose, except maybe to serve as some sort of a cautionary tale for others. On the other hand, my probation officer said at the time, "Obstacles are sometimes opportunities for growth." As we all know, life is defined by successes and setbacks. The ability to bounce back from failures is a defining factor in achieving one's goals. Putting it into a different perspective, the French philosopher Michel de Montaigne proclaimed, "There are some defeats more triumphant than victories," and certainly more instructive.

EPILOGUE

A week after the reunion, I met Howie at our favorite diner for lunch. When I got there, I wasn't the least surprised that Howie was already seated, almost unable to talk, lips puckering, in the eager anticipation of confiding the details of his meeting with Carol, or so I thought. However, I soon learned, Howie could barely get his words out, even had trouble speaking, because his mouth was stuffed with sour pickles the waiter had provided.

Howie, wiping his pickle-juice-filled mouth with a napkin, muttered, "Thanks for coming, good to see ya. I started without ya, as you can see. Boy, these pickles have some kick to them—really tart. You better grab the last one; otherwise, I might get sick. It would be my fourth."

Grimacing after taking a bite, I said, "I had a blast at the reunion, couldn't believe how fast it flew by. It was great seeing so many classmates. There's nothing better than old friends, literally. I had a great time, but I'm sure it was nothing compared to your night. Couldn't help noticing you two the whole night. Are you guys married yet? So tell me what happened. By the way, see ya still have a thing for pickles."

"Where'd we leave off?" Howie asked.

"You were going back to Carol after Kramer took some photos of the guys we hung out with," I said.

"Oh, yeah, I remember now. I finally went up to her, our eyes met, and I just froze, couldn't speak at all. Then, after what seemed like an eternity, I remember asking her some absolutely asinine question, like how ya doing or something like that." While watching Howie smile away as he recalled the moment, I couldn't stop grinning myself, seeing how Howie's face light up.

Howie resumed, "I racked my brains trying to think of something meaningful to say, but didn't know where to start. My mind went blank, resulting in this awkward silence. Trying to go forward by reaching back to yesteryear, I wondered if I should've apologized for being the one who ended our relationship. I knew she was badly hurt, and I agonized over the right words, though what I wanted to convey, was more than words could say.

"Standing next to her, I almost trembled like a child, like a bundle of energy surging with adrenaline. Every memory and feeling resurfaced, flooding back as if it were yesterday. A half hour later, after some of the nervousness and trepidation subsided, I blurted, 'You were the only girl I ever loved. No other woman, including my ex-wife, ever came close to how I felt about you…'"

Yep, there was a pause.

"Teary-eyed, watching her mascara redesign her face, she took my hand and said, 'I'm amazed after fifty years you still feel this way. That's either wonderful or pathetic, depending how you look at it. You're making all those tears I've been trying to make disappear, reappear.' She giggled and stated, 'I guess things that were so important back then aren't as important as they once were.'

"I said, 'Being with you makes me feel so alive, I don't remember the last time I've felt this way. I just want to be with you and enjoy the years we have left. A philosopher (G. Whyte-Melville) said, 'We always believe our first love is our last and our last love is our first.' Carol, it just so happens you're one and the same, so I guess I'll have to come up with some new quote.'"

Listening to the passion and excitement in Howie's portrayal of the two lovebirds' renewed romance was unquestionably heart-warming. The fact Howie took my advice and had the guts to open up, exposing his innermost feelings, showed how much he wanted it to work. It also reinforces the concept: it's great to be in love at any age!

That night, after penning some of these lovey-dovey events (actually fingers to keyboard), I happened to come across a quote by John Burroughs that read, "I still find each day too short for all the thoughts I want to think, all the walks I want to take, all the books I want to read, and all the friends I want to see." As I reread the quote, as I often do when something jumps out at me, a James Taylor song played on the radio. Included in his song were the lyrics, "You lose a little life with every breath." Realizing my mind was running faster than my fingers, and as a result of these coincident, out-of-the-clear-blue-sky messages, the need to put this story to bed was clearly delivered. But before I do, I'll finish with this fitting unforeseen event.

LOVING ADDENDUM

As fate would have it, the next day after lunch with Howie, I was scheduled to extract a number of broken-down, abscessed teeth on an eighty-eight-year-old new patient. At the appointment, because his equally aged wife insisted, they wanted to again discuss their heightened concerns regarding his many major health issues, medications, and surgery. Aided by their walkers (in theory), they glacially inched their way into the treatment room, banging into everything in sight. Given that the patient couldn't completely stop his blood thinners because it might trigger a stroke, the couple was forewarned to expect moderate postsurgical bleeding. From the devoted couple's poignant, tender interactions, their love was self-evident. When my assistant attempted to usher his wife out, she lingered, stroked his almost nonexistent hair, and even might've shed a tear before kissing him on the cheek goodbye. It was obvious both were more than a little worried. This aged dentist, who's human at times, was fully aware of the magnitude of their apprehension.

The multiple extractions and suturing went well. Prior to the postextraction instructions, I asked my assistant to summon the patient's visibly worried wife back into the operatory. This is a no-brainer because of the patient's age; I always assume four ears are better than two. After giving the postsurgical instructions and dying to know how long they've been together, I asked, "So how long have you two lovebirds been married?"

Anticipating a much greater number, I was blown away when the spouse cheerfully let me know, "Eighteen years. We got together at our fiftieth high school reunion. We dated through Riverhead High but then lost track. We both lost our spouses to cancer, but when we stumbled into one another at the reunion, our flames reignited the moment we laid eyes on each other."

Somewhere I read this hopeful, consoling thought: "As time goes by, love grows quieter. Passion may wane, but love, I've been told, is more solid the closer you get to the end" (anonymous).